Liz Flower is a writer and editor who has run her own bookshop specializing in Eastern and Western mysticism, psychology, astrology and related subjects. She has been interested in world religions since childhood and, in addition to working on other publishing projects, continues to research into this area.

The *Elements Of* is a series designed to present high-quality introductions to a broad range of essential subjects.

The books are commissioned specifically from experts in their fields. They provide readable and often unique views of the various topics covered, and are therefore of interest both to those who have some knowledge of the subject, as well as to those who are approaching it for the first time.

Many of these concise yet comprehensive books have practical suggestions and exercises which allow personal experience as well as theorectical understanding, and offer a valuable source of information on many important themes.

In the same series

The Aborigine Tradition
Alchemy
The Arthurian Tradition
The Bahá'í Faith
Astrology
Buddhism
Celtic Christianity
The Chakras
Christian Symbolism
Creation Myth
Dreamwork
The Druid Tradition
Earth Mysteries
Egyptian Wisdom
Feng Shui
Gnosticism
The Goddess
The Grail Tradition
Graphology
Handreading
Herbalism
Hinduism
Human Potential
The I Ching
Islam
Judaism
Meditation
Mysticism
Native American Traditions
Natural Magic
Numerology
Pendulum Dowsing
Prophecy
Psychosynthesis
The Qabalah
Reincarnation
The Runes
Shamanism
Sufism
Tai Chi
Taoism
The Tarot
Visualisation
Yoga
Zen

the elements of

world religions

Liz Flower

Shaftesbury, Dorset • Rockport, Massachusetts • Melbourne, Victoria

First published in Great Britain in 1997 by
Element Books Limited
Shaftesbury, Dorset SP7 8BP

Published in the USA in 1997 by
Element Books, Inc
PO Box 830, Rockport, MA 01966

Published in Australia in 1997 by
Element Books
and distributed by Penguin Australia Limited
487 Maroondah Highway, Ringwood, Victoria 3134

Cover design by Max Fairbrother
Page design by Roger Lightfoot
Typeset by Backup Creative Services, Dorset DT10 1DB
Printed and bound in Great Britain by
Biddles Ltd, Guildford & Kings Lynn

British Library Cataloguing in Publication
data available

Library of Congress Cataloguing in Publication data
Flower Liz.
The Elements of World Religions/Liz Flower.
p. cm. — (The elements of)
Includes bibliographical references and index
ISBN 1–86204–128–8 (pbk. alk. paper)
1. Religions I. Title. II. Series.
BL80.2.F58 1997
291—dc21
97–27901 CIP
ISBN 1–86204–128–8

CONTENTS

ACKNOWLEDGEMENTS

With thanks to all those people who put up with me for the duration, but most particularly to John Baldock, without whose active encouragement, guidance, fine-tuning and superb editing this would never have been finished.

INTRODUCTION

Mankind has experienced an urge toward religion and spirituality since the beginning of time. But what is religion? Taken from the Latin stem *religio*, it essentially means a bond between ourselves and the gods, meaning a (mutual) obligation between one and the other, and a due reverence for the gods. Within the context of this book religion means either 1) a particular system of faith and worship as practised by a group of people, or more broadly, 2) a recognition that people look for something outside themselves, a higher power that guides and controls, some superior being that they can revere and obey. Religions have either the one all-powerful God (Judaism, Christianity, Islam, Sikhism), or a pantheon of gods within which the One may be implicit (Hinduism, Shinto, primal religions), or indeed no God as such, but a state of transcendence with which one may escape from the sufferings of the world (Buddhism, Jainism) by following the teachings of the first propounder (and his successors) of that religion.

Within the context of the first meaning 'religion' also denotes a specific set of beliefs and practices, which are unique to each. It is mostly in these outward forms that religions differ. Many of the rituals in a religious service or observance are re-enactments of the central myth or myths surrounding the basic beliefs of that religion. With some countries and creeds division between religion and state is total, in others it is indivisible. Some have hierarchies imposed by the institutionalization of religion (in particular Christianity), so that intercession with God is handled mostly by priests. Some place no hierarchical priesthood between the worshipper and God (Islam). Others encourage, even demand (Hinduism), the involvement of all in their rituals – this makes them totally part of the Hindu community. But the common thread of seeking transcendence and desire for union with God, cosmos or universe is one that pervades all religions. It is important to recognize that, for the end result is the same. Even if the method of getting there is different.

Why is religion important? Religion gives people a sense of their place in the cosmos. There is evidence in the archaeological remains of prehistoric man that there were some forms of primitive worship and signs of fertility rites in later civilizations; indicating a desire for help and comfort from other than human sources.

Throughout history human faith in a god or gods has been kept alive in spite of rigorous repression and persecution. The need for something in which to believe seems to be fundamental to the human condition. Most human beings feel the need to believe in something (even if it is just making money, or the complete redecoration of the house annually), as well as the need to conform and belong (societies, communities, clubs), plus a need to escape (holidays, sleep, suicide). Any religion is, in varying degrees, compounded of exactly these three: faith (in a god, gods or other similar presence), a need to belong and a desire to escape. Loss or absence of faith does not necessarily mean the loss or absence of religion, just a change of emphasis. The sense of belonging provided by religion is indicated in the shared experiences of ritual in the face of death and suffering, and in the rites and mores of daily life and worship. As for escape: this is a deep-rooted desire for spiritual peace, for harmony with the divinity; by solitary contemplation and meditation at one end of the scale, and by populous, rowdy, joyous prayer meetings at the other.

Within each religion there are those that aspire towards the mystical union with God. This is usually done by setting oneself apart from the mainstream and by denying oneself anything but the most basic necessities, and sometimes not even those. Christianity has had its fair share of saints of this sort, as has Islam – except that in Islam the Sufis, except for a very few totally ascetic beings, prefer to live in the world to pass on their knowledge. The Sufis, in essence, seem to combine practicality with numinosity. The opposite end of the pole is fundamentalism, in which the strictest adherence to the Word, whatever it happens to be, and wherever it came from, is of paramount importance. It is taken as literal truths, with no room allowed for mystical ideas for liberal interpretation. No deviation is allowed from the path, otherwise severe punishment will ensue.

The wide range of cultural, social and geographical divergences means that there is no one religion that can satisfy the religious or spiritual needs of all the world's people. As a result, even individual religions in the course of their evolution have divided into numerous sects or branches. Christianity, for instance, is split into Catholic, Roman Catholic, Anglican, Protestant, Eastern and Greek Orthodox, Oriental; plus, under the Protestant banner, for example, Baptist, Presbyterian, Methodist, Quaker, Non-Conformist. Within these there are others also. Islam is mainly divided into two sects, Sunni and Shi'a. The Bahá'í faith, once an Islamic sect (and still being persecuted in Iran), is now regarded as a worldwide religion. Buddhism (with its origins in Hinduism) has Theravada and Mahayana, as well as Tibetan, Chinese and Japanese forms.

A sect is different from a cult in that a sect is part of the mainstream religion, and does observe (mostly) the scriptures that are part of that religion. The interpretations may differ, it may choose to emphasize some aspects and disregard others, and thus become fairly exclusive, but usually the fundamentals of both breakaway sect and orthodox religion tend to remain the same. Today, figures show that certain sects are gaining more members than the orthodox institutions, probably because they appear to engender a greater sense of belonging.

A cult may be a breakaway from the mainstream, or it may be founded on some premise unknown in any orthodox faith. A cult tends to be founded by one exceptionally charismatic person, who has a personal, usually aberrant, interpretation of some aspect of a scripture or a theological position. This person usually has a direct line to God (sometimes claiming to be God himself), and this God is usually neither loving nor benign, but punishing and wrathful. There is something of a proliferation of cults today, whose leader or leaders exert a phenomenal amount of hold over their followers, so much so that it leads to disaster – witness the cyanide gas release on the subway in Tokyo, or the shoot-out at Waco in Texas in 1993.

Religions today need to be balanced. The theology and cosmology as demonstrated by the earlier aspects of most of them are not necessarily relevant today. Christianity has probably had the fewest problems in coming to terms with the rapid spread of technology throughout the world, with some of Asian religions finding it most difficult. In some places technology has become the new religion and has undoubtedly given rise to a new wave of fundamentalism in religion worldwide, as the old order sees itself and its values under attack. All religions have the capacity to adapt, they just need the will. Finding out about the past helps us to understand how a particular religion works today: in effect, the two are inseparable. The study of a living religion can only be enhanced by knowledge of its history.

In this book I have tried to give a basic guide to the history, beliefs, scripture, doctrine, ritual and evolution of each religion. But that formula is not strict. One can approach religion from a theological point of view, or from a human, or sociological, or moral stance. People, whether theologians or laymen, will never agree on any one aspect of any religion, but at least one can go part way to understanding it. To those who would say that the study of religion is a waste of time, I would argue that anything that has the capability to move people as does religion – whether it be wise/foolish, good/evil, justified or not – is worth the study. Even, *must* be studied if there is any hope of comprehending some of the complexities that govern our many and varied responses to life. But most of all – an understanding of the world's religions can lead to an understanding of the universal truths that lie at the heart of all religions, and from there to a greater understanding between the peoples of the world.

1 • MONOTHEISM AND THE PROPHETIC TRADITION

JUDAISM

Judaism is the oldest of the revealed religions, with a history going back over 4,000 years. Its origins are discernible in the religion of Abraham – indeed there is an unbroken thread of belief and understanding reaching from those ancient times to the present day. The faith has had the most extraordinary capacity for survival, in spite of the trials of conquest, exile, discrimination and slaughter that have attended its path through history. This lies in the belief that they are one people: chosen by God to be an example of light and love to all mankind, and guided by an ethical monotheism whose foundations were laid in the time of the Patriarchs, and elaborated through the Torah – the Divine Teachings as revealed to Moses.

The heart of the Jewish faith is the belief in the One God, the Creator and Ruler of all. He is eternal and transcendent, and he alone is to be worshipped. He communicates to man through prophecy and Moses is regarded as the greatest of the prophets. God revealed the Torah (the Teaching) to Moses on Mount Sinai. The Torah (the five books of Moses, or the first five books of the Hebrew Bible: Genesis, Exodus, Leviticus, Numbers and Deuteronomy) is the ultimate, unchanging word of the Divine Law. God is all-knowing and all-seeing in his concern for man and he alone rewards or punishes. He will one day send a Messiah, a descendant of the line of David, who will usher in the age of redemption and the resurrection of the dead.

These thirteen fundamental beliefs were posited in the twelfth century CE by Maimonides, one of Judaism's greatest philosophers. But to convey the true essence of these beliefs and what it is that has bound so many people to these teachings over such a long time, it is necessary to look at the story of the Jewish people, their history and their relationships with other cultures.

THE HISTORY OF JUDAISM

Now the Lord had said unto Abram, Get thee out of thy country, and from thy kindred, and from thy father's house, unto a land that I will shew thee. And I will make of thee a great nation, and I will bless thee, and make thy name great: and thou shalt be a blessing; And I will bless them that bless thee and curse him that curseth thee; and in thee shall all families of the earth be blessed.

Genesis 12:1–3

This, some 2,000 BCE, was the first covenant with God: they would be his people and serve him and he would be their God. It was made by one of the nomadic Hebrew tribes under the leadership of Abraham. The covenant laid down the first rules and obligations of living in a right and just manner, in accordance with the will of God. It also promised a land, Canaan, that would belong to the tribes of Israel in perpetuity. This vision of a promised land is something that has been central to the Jewish ideal ever since.

Some six centuries later Moses reaffirmed the covenant on Mount Sinai. Moses is the foundation of the rabbinical tradition of Judaism. Moses led the enslaved Israelite tribe of Levi out of Egypt back to the land of Canaan (although he died before they reached it), and it is this flight from Egypt that is celebrated and remembered by the annual festival of Pesach, Passover. The term Torah covers all aspects of Jewish life and worship. The festival of Shavuot, or Pentecost, commemorates the giving of Torah on Mount Sinai. The Torah is not only the Teachings contained in the Pentateuch (the first five books of the Hebrew Bible), but it also refers to the oral teachings received by Moses. In its wider sense it is also the Law which binds those that follow its precepts to God.

At the time there was a plurality of gods, whose images were worshipped by the other peoples in and around Canaan. The notion that God was universal and for all peoples was yet to come. He was still an exclusive God, to be worshipped as the One by the followers of Moses, but never to be represented by idols and images. This has had a profound effect through the centuries – the Jewish God has never been represented in pictures. Words have been his medium and words have been the conveyors of divine truth.

Eventually, the kingdom of Judah was established in the land of Canaan and Solomon built the first temple in 950 BCE. The temple was the only place where Jewish ritual and sacrifice could be executed. Every Judean had a duty to make a pilgrimage to the temple in Jerusalem. This was made impossible in the first dispersion in 586 BCE when Nebuchadnezzar sacked Jerusalem, destroyed the temple and all the people were taken into Babylon in captivity.

In exile, the Jews began to set up places where they could meet, discuss and teach the Law, pray and read – the foundations of the synagogue. In this way they kept their faith, and their separateness, alive.

Cyrus the Great conquered Babylon some fifty years later, and the Jewish priests were allowed, eventually, to return to Jerusalem. Seventy years after the sacking of the temple by Nebuchadnezzar, it was rebuilt, and so was the domination of the priests. It is from this time that certain elements that enshrine the difference between Jew and non-Jew were made clear – particularly by the prophets Ezra and Nehemiah. These were circumcision (a rite carried out since the time of Abraham), observance of the Sabbath and of the Jewish Year, conformance to the Torah, marriage only within the faith and the obligation of every Jew to the temple. At the same time, the meetings in the synagogues continued to grow under the auspices of the scribes whose business it was not only to write down the scriptures, but to understand and interpret them. These scribes were the forerunners of the teachers, the rabbis. The advantage of the synagogue was that the Jewish faith could not only be practised anywhere – and was – but provided a focus too. The temple at Jerusalem, the priests, and the sacrificial rites were still pre-eminent.

The domination of the Greeks in the four centuries BCE contributed much both to Jewish dispersal and to Jewish thought, although it never altered the Torah. Communities of Jews still remained in Babylon and spread to other areas of the Hellenistic world, such as Alexandria and Antioch and Asia Minor.

Jerusalem and Judah suffered somewhat under the hands of certain Greek rulers – taxes, restrictions, the outside appointment of priests – but managed to retain a modicum of freedom. In 63 BCE Rome conquered the area and imposed its own governors. For a hundred or so years there were revolts, many of which centred on the Jewish hope of the Messiah, who was imminently expected.

The final act in the break-up of the country of Judah and of the priestly dominance of Judaism was the sacking of the temple in Jerusalem in 70 CE. The centre of Judaism was gone, to be replaced for ever by the synagogue. Jews found that they were small, if close-knit, groups within larger communities. Wherever they went, they would be affected from then on by whatever culture surrounded them. They could have been absorbed wholesale into new lands, but the Torah, the rise of the synagogue, and their belief in their faith and the precepts it stood for, kept their identity intact.

The Flowering of Jewish Medieval Philosophy

Over the next few centuries Jewish communities spread throughout the Christian countries of Europe and into the Islamic countries of the Middle East and North Africa. There have even been tales of Jewish pockets as far away as China. The next great flowering of Jewish thought and philosophy came in the Medieval period. It threw up philosophers such as Maimonides and the poet Halevi; a confluence of Aristotelian and Jewish thought; the mysteries of the Kabbalah which influenced the eighteenth-century Hasidic movement. It was a time for the teachers and thinkers to reconcile the difficulty of strict biblical texts with the modern world around them.

Maimonides (1135–1204) formulated the thirteen articles of faith, and is honoured by the Orthodox for his disquisitions on ritual and Law. His best-known work is 'The Guide for the Perplexed', in which he managed to combine the theory that the world is uncreated and everlasting with the theory that it was created by God, out of nothing. The Christian philosopher Thomas Aquinas was profoundly influenced by him. The polar opposite of Maimonides's intellectual pietism was the poet Yehudah Halevi, who believed in the transforming miracle of faith and the utter historicity of the Jews with their God and with their country.

In spite of the surge of intellectual thought during the Medieval period, and the later possibilities of the Enlightenment, the Jews remained in their ghettos, either barely tolerated or at worst, persecuted and driven out. For the diaspora of these Jewish communities the Medieval period came to an end only in the eighteenth and nineteenth centuries. This presents both the positive and negative aspects of separateness – the first is maintained in the pureness of belief and community, the second exhibited in the natural fear of differentness. This fear manifested itself over the years and in many different countries in pogroms and massacres. Jews were often offered the choice of conversion (either to Christianity or Islam, depending on the country), exile or death. Sometimes they were offered no choice.

THE JEWISH SCRIPTURES

Torah is the most common term both for the revelation from God and for the holy scriptures. It is the medium of God's will toward his people and the instruction of how they are to live their lives and worship him in both the inner and outer sense.

In its most narrow sense Torah refers to the Pentateuch. It is also the Teaching – God's injunction to his peoples, it is also the Law, and the lore of the Jews. Study of Torah is always necessary for new insights into the word of God, and to apply them to life today. Orthodoxy requires that nothing be changed, Torah is sacrosanct, immutable, but Reform Judaism is laxer in attitude.

Torah is also used for the oral scriptures, codified in the Mishnah, edited by Judah the Prince in the second century CE. The Mishnah is divided into six sections, dealing with the legal and ritual (halakhah) side of things: agricultural laws, festivals, the place of women, property and civil matters, the temple and ritual purity. Much of later Judaism is based on the Mishnah.

The Talmud (of which there are two versions, the more detailed and complete fifth-century CE Babylonian Talmud, and the fourth-century Palestinian Talmud) is second only to Torah as the main text of rabbinical (as opposed to temple) Judaism. It is made up of the Mishnah and the Gemara (commentaries on the Mishnah). The Talmud is encyclopedic both on the halakhah contents and on the aggadah, the theological, ethical and folkloric side of things, and rabbis often refer to it. Because the Talmud records all views, no matter who said it and why, there continues to be disputation and discussion by the knowledgeable. Commentaries known as Midrash (a tradition of rabbinical biblical exposition and exegesis designed to reveal the inner meaning of Torah) are often consulted, particularly when trying to reconcile contradictory texts. Today, the Shulhan Aruch, a sixteenth-century abridgement, is popularly used by most Jews, leaving the full Talmud for the scholars.

The Kabbalah is the mystical side of Judaism. It posited the connectedness of all things, and the divine and intimate correspondences between God and man. Man is God made manifest, because God is so hidden from us that he can only be seen in his correspondences. Ritual is the contact point — man, in his observance and prayer, may also effect harmony above, just as above gives joy to the worshipper. The Kabbalistic book is the Zohar, the Book of Splendours. It teaches that the world came into being through the ten sefirot (from *sefirah*, emanation), which are the manifestations of different aspects of God. According to Jewish mystical thought 'the sefirot depict both the creative outflow from God and the ladder of ascent by which the individual climbs towards the absolute'. The diagrammatic representation of the sefirot is known as the 'tree of sefirot' or the 'tree of life'. Some see the Kabbalah as the third book of Jewish scriptures after the Bible and the Talmud.

JEWISH BELIEF AND TRADITION

Tradition holds that a child is a Jew if born of a Jewish mother. For a boy, initiation into Judaism begins at eight days old with circumcision. As soon as a Jewish child can speak he learns the words of the Shema:

Hear, O Israel, the Lord our God is one Lord. And thou shalt love the Lord thy God with all thine heart, with all thy soul and with all thy might, And these words, which I shall command thee this day, shall be in thy heart. And thou shalt teach them diligently unto thy children, and shalt talk of them when thou sittest in thine house, and when thou walkest by the way, and when thou liest down and when thou risest up. And thou shalt bind them for a sign upon thine hand, and they shall be as frontlets before thine eyes. And thou shalt write them upon the posts of thy house and on thy gates.

Deuteronomy 6:4-9

These words affirm both the love of God and the love of serving God and are the cornerstone of belief and prayer in the Jewish community. The Shema is said during prayers, at night and by the dying. Some say them before approaching almost everything in daily life, thus bringing the numinosity of God into the practical.

At thirteen the boy enters into adulthood with his Bar Mitzvah, girls at twelve with their Bat Mitzvah. From then they partake fully in the life of a Jew. They eat only kosher food which conforms to their dietary laws. Only certain kinds of meat (no pig), which has been killed in such a manner as to rid the fibres of all blood, and fish (not shellfish) may be prepared. No milk may be taken with meat. Dietary observance varies from the non-existent to the severe. Blessings are recited before each meal.

Devout Jews pray three times a day, either at home or in the synagogue. The Orthodox wear a yarmulka (skullcap) and the prayer shawl – both marks of reverence. Phylacteries, the small boxes that contain four passages, including the Shema, from the Bible, may be worn on the forehead and upper arm. The Shema is also held in the mezuzah, a scroll in a box fixed to the front door and all the other doors in the house.

The Shabbat is the weekly religious festival. It celebrates the creation of the world and the delivery of the slaves from Egypt. From sunset on the Friday to sunset on the Saturday no work nor travel is permitted. Candles are lit to commemorate the light of God, the light of the world and the light of the faith, and also because in an Orthodox house, no one may switch on a lamp or light a fire. The Shabbat is, as well as a time for prayer and remembrance, also a time for eating and drinking and being jolly.

The synagogue must be within walking distance, because no one may drive on the Shabbat. On the wall that faces Jerusalem there is an ark, or cupboard, in which the Pentateuch is kept. During the Shabbat service it is taken out, paraded and read. A cantor may lead the service – the duties of a rabbi are to teach and instruct his congregation in the religion and to decide on points of Jewish law.

Marriage usually takes place in the synagogue. Marriage is considered one of the duties of a Jew – it means the start of a new family, and families are the basis of Judaism. The bride and groom are considered to be making a holy covenant. The ceremony includes the breaking of a glass to remind everyone that there is always sadness amid joy.

Death has its rituals, too. Burial should take place as soon and as simply as possible, and kaddish, a prayer in praise of God, is said in memory. The mourning is ritualized, being intense for the first week after death, and gradually lessening, giving time for the bereft to grieve but also to make sure there is no self-indulgence. On the anniversary of a parent's death, the children light a candle and recite kaddish at the end of the service in the synagogue.

The Jewish Year starts in September or October with Rosh Hashanah. As the Hebrew prayer book says, 'This is the day the world was called into existence. This day He causeth all creatures to stand in judgement.' A ram's horn is blown in the synagogue to call the congregation and remind them of their shortcomings, and ten days are spent in repentance.

At the end of the ten days is Yom Kippur, the Day of Atonement. This is the holiest day of the Jewish year. People fast for twenty-five hours, no comforts – material or sexual – are allowed and much of the time is spent in the synagogue confessing. It is based on the days when priests made sacrifice in the temple to atone for the sins of the people of Israel. At the end of the day the sinner is deemed to have repented and been forgiven by God.

Five days later is the Feast of the Tabernacles (Sukkot). This is a week-long joyous harvest festival which celebrates the people's return to Canaan after forty years of wandering in the wilderness having fled from Egypt. At the end of Sukkot come the Rejoicing of the Torah, Simchat Torah, when the yearly cycle of reading from the Pentateuch is begun again with the Book of Genesis.

In December is the Festival of Lights, Hanukkah. This commemorates the victory of Judas Maccabaeus in the second century BCE and the rededication of the temple in Jerusalem. This eight-day festival centres around the daily lighting of the menorah, the seven-branched candlestick. One candle is lit each day by the 'servant', the eighth candle, until all are alight on the eighth day.

Purim falls in February or March. It is a time for parties, often in fancy dress, and for sending gifts of food. The Book of Esther is read in the synagogue, and it celebrates how the

Jews were saved during the time of the Persian Empire, from Haman, who was plotting the deaths of them all. The congregation boo and stamp their feet every time Haman's name is read out.

A month later, March or April, is Pesach (Passover) – the best known of all the Jewish festivals. This recalls the safe delivery of the people from Egypt. Matzah bread and bitter herbs are eaten (a reminder of the hard times in Egypt and during the flight). No leavened, yeast-risen bread may be eaten during the festival; indeed no yeast or leaven may be retained in the house. There is a ritual meal (the seder) held on the first night at which the youngest member of the family asks, 'Why is this night different from all other nights?' This is the cue for the father to read the story of Exodus from the special Haggadah (story or storytelling) text. Even Jews who do not follow traditional ways in any sense tend to celebrate Pesach. It is a special celebration of family ties, even in a faith that holds the family in high esteem.

Pesach is followed by seven weeks of semi-mourning, ending with Pentecost, or Shavuot. This is the time when Moses received the Ten Commandments, which are read in the synagogue. Many Jews stay up all the first night in the study of the Torah. Shavuot is also known as the Feast of First Fruits, the first harvest of the year. Five weeks after Pentecost come another three weeks of mourning, when the destruction of the temple in 70 CE by the Romans is remembered. This starts with a fast and ends also, on Tisha B'av, in July or August. It is not only the tearing down of the temple that is remembered, but the suffering endured by the Jews in various places and times ever since.

JUDAISM TODAY

During the eighteenth century it became apparent for many communities that to continue the Jewish isolation in the ghetto would alienate them beyond repair from the world outside. This was certainly obvious in those Jewish communities which left Eastern Europe for the richer grounds of Western Europe or for the new country of America.

Moses Mendelssohn (1729–86) was influential in the notion of Emancipation and the forerunner of the movement for Reform. He, in turn, had been influenced by reading Maimonides. He advocated religious tolerance and separation of church and state; he urged both that Judaism was a rational universal religion and that being Jewish was not a nationality but a religion only. A Jew could be a loyal citizen of any country, and follow his own religion. Mendelssohn's work, along with the new egalitarian movements generated by the French Revolution, were deeply instrumental in the great explosion of Jewish creativity throughout Europe. Many Jews became assimilated into their countries, aware of their roots, but no longer adhering to strict Judaism.

Reform was a response to, and a consequence of, this gradual emancipation. The Age of Reason, progress and scientific inquiry provoked thought of sweeping changes in Judaism. A prime mover was Abraham Geiger (1810–74), who put forward changes to worship in the synagogue and in ritual and dietary law. To accept the revelation of the Torah as fact was an impossibility in such a scientific age. The Reform movement became particularly influential in America under the guidance of Rabbi Isaac Wise (1819–1900). The Reform movement today is still evolving, still the most liberal branch of Judaism. It emphasizes the ethics of the faith rather than the ritual law. Propositions should stand, not because they have been ordained by God, but because they have relevance to the here and now.

But not everyone was happy with such progressive and radical changes. The Conservative movement was born in Europe, but has held sway mostly in America, where it has become the largest group among Jewish believers. This branch wished for changes that were compatible with historical development. Tradition was stressed, but change had to be allowed in order for the Jews to preserve their national identity, which they felt was likely to be lost under Reform Judaism. The Conservative school also gave birth in the twentieth century to Reconstructionism, which considers Judaism to be constantly evolving.

In complete contrast to both the Reform and Conservative branches, Hasidism, founded in the late eighteenth century by Israel Baal Shem Tov (1700–60), is based on the mystical rather that the ritual. It takes its teachings from the Kabbalah and insists that God is to be observed in every facet of life, not just through the Commandments. The resonance of the Hasidic Jew is the 'cleaving to God in joy', its emphasis on emotion and ecstatic devotion to God. Its appeal was immediate and it gained many followers. Originally regarded as heterodox, they were always in danger of excommunication. Today they are virtually indistinguishable from the orthodox, except they owe allegiance to their rebbe, whose word is absolute. There are many Hasidic sects all centred around one leader.

One of the most important movements that came out of this age was Zionism. In spite of emancipation, anti-Semitism was still rife, and at the turn of the century the overt prejudice of the Dreyfus case in France was the turning point for Theodor Herzl (1860–1904). Until then, he had considered assimilation the answer to any Jewish problem, but with anti-Jewishness in the open again he turned his thoughts to the old dream of a Jewish homeland. Herzl is considered the father of political Zionism, the creation of a Jewish state through politics rather than by any agency of the supernatural. He chaired the first conference in Basle in 1897. His vision was of a secular state, not ruled by the religion or rabbinic law, but a state bound together through a shared history and national identity.

The anti-Semitism that prompted Herzl grew in strength until it culminated in the Nazi holocaust, when over six million Jews were put to death in gas chambers. This was profoundly shocking for those outside Judaism, but for those who professed the faith it was devastating. It was not only the deaths of so many people, but also the depth of prejudice behind it. The need for an Israeli state became paramount – not just as the fulfilment of the promise made by God to Abraham and Moses 4,000 years earlier, but as a question of safety. The state of Israel was set up on 14 May 1948. This has indeed given the Jewish nation, physically and spiritually, creatively and culturally, a renewed sense of who they are and where they came from.

CHRISTIANITY

At the heart of Christianity is the figure of Jesus Christ: God, man, icon. Christ comes from the Greek, *Khristos*, a translation of the Hebrew *māshīah* ('anointed one'), which is the name Jesus came to be known by when the incipient faith of Christianity was being carried abroad by the early teachers. For Christians, Christ is the human face of God. As he said, 'I am the way, and the truth and the life; no one comes to the Father but by me.' And it is through following the example of his life and teachings that Christians are able to draw close to the ineffable mystery of God.

THE LIFE OF JESUS

It is now widely accepted that Jesus was born around 4 BCE in Bethlehem, Galilee, and was crucified 33 years later in Jerusalem. The details of his life are recorded in the Gospels of Matthew, Mark, Luke and John, but of the events that transpired between his miraculous birth – his divine conception, the virgin birth, the wise men following the star, the angelic annunciation to the shepherds – and the start of his ministry some years later, virtually nothing is known. Only one incident from these intervening years is mentioned in Luke: at the age of 12 Jesus became separated from his parents – Mary and Joseph – while visiting Jerusalem. After much searching, his anxious parents eventually found him in the temple. His response to their concern reveals his sense of divine purpose: 'How is it that you sought me? Did you not know that I must be in my father's house?'

Jesus' ministry started with his baptism by John, after which he spent 40 days in the desert (like the ancient prophets) before beginning to preach. When John was imprisoned he returned to Galilee and gathered round him a small band of followers. They adopted the life of wandering mendicants,

19

homeless, dependent on charity. The Gospels portray his ministry as one of healing, teaching and preaching. He also performed many miracles, such as the multiplication of loaves and fishes, raising Lazarus from the dead, changing water into wine at a marriage feast, and calming the storm on the Sea of Galilee.

His message was simple: 'The time is fulfilled, the kingdom of God is at hand: repent ye, and believe in the Gospel' (Mark 1:15). He gathered crowds wherever he preached, mostly because his preaching was direct and comprehensible to the ordinary Jew. He taught that a new age was dawning when the reign of God would be supreme. God's will was ultimate. Everyone should have faith in his powers: faith and obedience to his will were the essences of love and understanding of God, which would lead to walking in the ways of God. By accepting the will of God, all might enter into the kingdom, but only if the Jews repented and returned to their true loyalty to God. But as time went by it became obvious that the Jews were rejecting his call, so Jesus began to open his ministry to Gentiles and to others who were regarded as unacceptable. His unconventional approach may be summed up in his words: 'The first shall be last and the last shall be first.'

His popularity among Jew and Gentile alike, as well as his iconoclastic attitude towards religious questions roused the antipathy of both the Pharisees (who adhered deeply to the legality of Judaism) and the Saducees, who were the priestly rulers. Jesus proclaimed that purity of heart was infinitely more important than ritual cleansing. It was the thoughts that man had which drove him to evil – not eating with unwashed hands. This was an abhorrent idea for the Pharisees. For the Saducees, whose powers depended on Rome, Jesus' following posed a greater problem – possible revolution. Was he the promised King of the Jews? His popularity with the people appeared to say so.

But Jesus did not see himself as the Messiah as it was popularly understood. He was not a political Messiah, nor a king to rule on earth – although it was urged on him more than once. When he made his Passover entrance into

Jerusalem on a humble donkey it was in the style of a ruler in service to his people. The enthusiastic crowd expected him to declare his kingship and rise against Rome. Instead he argued with the authorities and showed his contempt for the misuse of the temple. His insistence that the kingdom of God was not a literal and military proposition disillusioned many Jewish followers, including one of his disciples.

Even so, he was sufficiently dangerous in the eyes of the Jewish leaders for them to arrange to have him arrested with the help of the disillusioned Judas. He was charged, under Judaic law, with blasphemy: his 'claim' to be the Messiah and the Son of God. But they needed the sanction of the Roman rulers to pass the death sentence and gave insurrection as a reason. So Jesus was executed as the 'King of the Jews' and a popular political rebel – a final irony, considering that by his refusal to rise against Rome he lost the support of the people. His death was by crucifixion – a particularly vile, drawn-out method, used for rebels. His body was taken down by followers and placed in a tomb. The cross on which he was crucified came to stand as the symbol of his life, death and resurrection – a potent reminder of all that Jesus did for his followers.

It is in what happened next that the focus of Christianity is seen. Towards the end of his ministry, Jesus had announced that he expected to be killed and that through this act his disciples would understand both the need for this ultimate sacrifice and its significance of salvation. But to the disciples his death seemed pointless. Two days later they found the tomb empty and were even more puzzled. It was not until Jesus appeared to them several times, seemingly as corporeal as they, but not bound by the usual earthly limitations of walls and doors, that they began to understand. While he was alive they had seen him as a great teacher, while at the same time longing for the Messiah. It was only after his death that they recognised him for what he was.

He reiterated the reasons for his life and his death. He had come to 'minister, and to give his life a ransom for many' (Mark 10:45), whereby his death would free mankind from sin and would reconcile them with God, with whom they would then live in harmony. He was the ultimate, perfect sacrifice. After Jesus, no further sacrifice would be necessary. And his work, from then on, was to be undertaken by his disciples, who were also to proclaim Jesus as the Messiah – a state that was made possible only by his death and, finally and most importantly, by his resurrection. Ten days after the ascension of Jesus into heaven, the Holy Spirit of God is deemed to have endowed his followers with its power. This visitation enabled Jesus' disciples to continue his ministry, now invested with the Holy Spirit, allowing them to act as Jesus' representatives on earth.

THE TEACHINGS OF JESUS

Jesus' teaching is summed up in the Sermon on the Mount, which he preached to an enormous following. In its entirety it is a lengthy piece – here he advocates overturning the status quo as adhered to by Pharisee and Saducee.

Blessed are the pure in spirit: for theirs is the Kingdom of heaven.
Blessed are they that mourn: for they shall be comforted.
Blessed are the meek: for they shall inherit the earth.
Blessed are they which do hunger and thirst after righteousness: for they shall be filled.
Blessed are the merciful: for they shall obtain mercy.
Blessed are the pure in heart: for they shall see God.
Blessed are the peacemakers: for they shall be called the children of God.
Blessed are they which are persecuted for righteousness' sake: for theirs is the kingdom of heaven.
Blessed are ye, when men shall revile you, and persecute you, and shall say all manner of evil against you falsely, for my sake.
Rejoice, and be exceeding glad: for great is your reward in heaven: for so persecuted they the prophets which came before you.

Matthew 5:3–12

In the same sermon Jesus outlined the simple prayer to be said with reverence and humility. This is known as the Lord's Prayer, and is the staple of Christian services worldwide. Between this prayer and Jesus' exhortation of love (see below) may be found the distillation of all things Christian.

Our Father, which art in heaven, Hallowed be thy name. Thy kingdom come. Thy will be done in earth, as it is in heaven. Give us this day our daily bread, and forgive us our sins as we forgive those who sin against us. And lead us not into temptation, but deliver us from evil. For thine is the kingdom, and the power, and the glory, for ever. Amen.

Matthew 6:9–13

Jesus made much use of parables so that his teachings might be understood by everyone. He also reduced the Law of the Ten Commandments to two Commandments, the essence of which is also the essence of his teaching – and that is *unconditional* love.

Love the Lord thy God with all thy heart, with all thy soul, with all thy mind. This is the first and greatest commandment. And the second is like unto it: Love thy neighbour as thyself.

Matthew 22:37–40

THE CHRISTIAN SCRIPTURES

Next to the figure of Jesus, the Bible holds the place of honour among Christians. It is, in reality, a collection of books, written over more than 1,000 years, in a plurality of languages and styles. It is divided into two – unequal – parts: the Old and New Testaments. The Old Testament is the Judaic scripture, containing the history of the Jews and all the centuries of Hebrew thought to which Christians see themselves as heirs. The books are rich in story, fable, allegory and poetry. The word testament means a covenant, or bond, and the two Testaments, Old and New, outline this bond (relationship) with God in contrasting ways: the Old according to the Law, the New according to the Holy Spirit. Christians regard the New Testament as the fulfilment of the Old, because the figure of Jesus and the events of his life fulfil the prophecies of the coming of the Messiah.

The New Testament, written mostly during the first century CE consists of 27 books: the four Gospels of Matthew, Mark, Luke and John which delineate the life and teachings of Jesus; the Acts of the Apostles, in which the first 30 years of the church may be found; 21 letters by early Christian leaders to various communities and individuals, of which 13 were written by St Paul. The final book of the New Testament is the Revelation of St John the Divine, a work of apocalyptic vision.

The Bible is regarded as the arbiter of doctrine by the Christian Church and the place where the proper rules of church life are to be found. It is considered as 'inspired', meaning that although there is a multiplicity of authors and a variety of styles, what is written is thought to have come directly from God. Some take the writings to be absolute and true facts, others regard some of the stories, in both Testaments, as more allegorical and as demonstrating the essence of the infallibility both of God and of Jesus Christ.

Today the whole Bible is translated into over 300 languages, with the New Testament, and other parts, available in over 1,500 translations.

CHRISTIAN BELIEFS AND PRACTICES

Christianity is a monotheistic faith. It believes in the one God. This is complicated rather by the doctrine of the Trinity: the Father, Son and Holy Spirit.

How can a god be one and three at the same time? The answer was thrashed out in the fourth century, at the Council of Nicaea, that the one God is revealed in three persons: Father, Son and Holy Spirit. They are 'three persons in the same substance' and as such are united — but yet separate. None the less, it is not accepted by some branches of Christianity: nor by some theologians, who also have difficulty with the incarnation of Jesus as man. But part of the essence of a doctrine such as this is that it *should* be difficult and ungraspable — as God himself is. Attempts to explain the Trinity either by positing the Father as the only divinity or in terms of the Three being three different *aspects* of God takes away from his infinity, his unknowableness. The doctrine of the Trinity is best summarized in the Nicene Creed.

The beliefs of the Christian Church are that Jesus is divine, but was made man and came down to earth to carry out God's will; that he died for our sins and 'rose from the dead, having conquered sin and death', in the triumph of resurrection; that Christ is the Son of God, that he is part of the Three in One. Then, almost practically, the essence of Christ's death is salvation, which depends on the grace, the divine favour of God, shown in the atonement for man's sins by the death of Jesus Christ on the cross. And that Jesus, although divine, also walks with his followers on earth, that he is present in them and they in him, in their belief and trust.

It is in this last premise that he is perhaps most visible, that of Church and community. This is the vital, communal aspect of Christianity. 'Church' has three meanings: the actual building in which worship is held; the institution of the Church, as a regulatory body or an employer; and the community, or the people, united in the one faith. It is also referred to as 'the body of Christ', the representation of him on earth and in communion with his people; or as the 'bride of Christ', a distinct but linked separation, most often used in the Eastern Church. It is also the community of the Christian Church worldwide, an understanding that whatever the differences, all Christians are bound together in the one faith. The Nicene Creed calls it the 'one, holy, catholic and apostolic Church'.

Holy, because it is set aside for God, away from the sinful world. There were arguments that sinners should be excluded, but those who maintained that the Church was more for sinners than for saints held sway. This was rationalized eventually by Augustine, who posited that there was a Church 'visible' – those that could be seen worshipping, and a Church 'invisible' – those who were true Christians, and only God and the heart knew who.

Catholic is not used in the sense of Roman Catholic, but meaning universal. The church should always be available for everyone, worldwide. And finally, apostolic, because it held to the faith handed down by the twelve apostles of Jesus Christ.

Christian Ritual

Ritual and practice in the Christian Church is vast and varied. Most rites and rituals take place in church or chapel and are liturgy driven – a few, such as Quakers, are not. And because Christianity is highly syncretistic, there are many local forms.

All use prayer, either privately or publicly. It addresses God through his Son and calls on the Holy Spirit to work through the medium of prayer. It is both an act of love and dedication through obligation. It is also a privilege which allows some contact with transcendence. Private prayer may often be reserved for the meditative and the mystical in an approach to God. The Western Church is inclined less toward the mystical these days, although in its history there have been some truly notable mystics. The Eastern Church, on the other hand, still maintains an understanding of mysticism, indeed actively promotes it.

Public prayer is mostly clergy led. In the early days it was unstructured; a few people gathering together to pray, sing and teach. This developed over time into a system of bishops and priests who held the service and were the active communicants. The congregation were passive participants. It was not until the Reformation that ordinary worshippers were allowed to take Communion. Today there are moves in some quarters for more active participation.

Wherever Christian prayer is held it will include the Lord's Prayer. It is an affirmation of the doctrine and teachings of God. Most congregations sing hymns and psalms and use prayers from other sources as well.

Giving is a practice that all Christians are exhorted to follow. This means not only giving to the poor and needy, but also supporting the Church, its clergy and your local church.

The Sacraments

The Book of Common Prayer defines a sacrament as 'an outward and visible sign of an inward spiritual grace'. It is through the sacraments that God, through the Holy Spirit, is present in mankind. The Roman Church shares with the Eastern Churches a recognition of seven sacraments: baptism, confirmation, marriage, ordination, penance, anointing of the sick and, most especially, Mass. The Protestant Churches recognize only the two principal sacraments of Baptism and the Lord's Supper – Communion – as having been instituted by Jesus.

Baptism is the initiation into the Christian faith. It is associated, first, with repentance and faith and commitment and, second, with the arrival of the Holy Spirit. These days, in predominantly Christian countries, children are assumed to belong already to the corpus of Christianity and so are baptized as babies. They are expected, however, to make a profession of their commitment when they are old enough. Baptism used to mean total immersion and in some church denominations, and in some countries it still does. Mostly, however, it is a question of a small dribble of consecrated water on the head of the individual. The water signifies the public washing, or cleansing, and acceptance of the faith. Ritual cleansing with water is a rite so old its origins cannot be dated.

Communion has several names – Eucharist, the Lord's Supper, Mass – depending on the denomination. Most branches of the Church practise it; the Quakers are a notable exception and prefer to stress the internal aspects of devotion, rather than the external. Its origins lie in the Last Supper that Jesus ate with his disciples before his crucifixion. Bread (leavened in the East, unleavened in the West) is broken and eaten, and wine is drunk.

Some forms of Communion are highly ceremonial, others very simple. There are variations in whether the congregation kneel or sit, the participation of priests, the frequency of its occurrence and its meaning. Communion is considered, diversely, as the representation of the death of Christ, a symbolic expiation of sin, the embodiment of Christ in the bread and wine, an invocation of his presence, or a representation of Christ's sacrifice.

Confirmation is a lesser ritual. Where infant baptisms are predominant, confirmation is designed to show acceptance of the Christian ethics and the community. These days, in the Protestant church for instance, it is done by the laying on of hands which signifies, again, the endowment of the Holy Spirit.

Christian Festivals

Easter is the major festival in the Christian calendar, at least in the Church. Easter occurs sometime during March and April and commemorates the resurrection of Jesus Christ. It coincides nearly with the Jewish Passover. In the Eastern Church, the whole weekend is a time for rejoicing, placing emphasis on the triumph over death. In the West, the day of the crucifixion (Good Friday), is one of sadness followed by the joy of the risen Christ at Easter.

The largest festival in the eyes of the public, however, is Christmas, celebrating the nativity of Jesus. This festival, on 25 December, is an appropriation by the Church of the old pagan midwinter festival. It is a time for families, gifts, feasting and carol singing.

During the rest of the year the other observances in the Christian calendar are:

Advent, in November/December, the preparation both for Christmas, in secular terms, and the preparation by the church for the birth of Christ.

Lent, in February and April, are 40 days which correspond both to Jesus' 40 days in the wilderness before taking up his ministry, and to the 40 years that the Jews spent wandering back from exile in Egypt. It is a period of fasting and of abstinence.

Forty days after Easter is Ascension Day, celebrating Jesus' ascension into heaven. Ten days later is Pentecost, the day God sent the Holy Spirit to all Jesus' apostles; this day celebrates the birth of the Church.

Christians celebrate Sunday — the first day of the week. Taking the Mosaic law as the injunction for a day of rest, the newly formed Christian community chose Sunday, partly to differentiate themselves from the Jewish Shabbat and also because the day is associated with Christ's resurrection. It became the day when all duties of holiness were required.

THE HISTORY OF CHRISTIANITY

The history of Christianity is long and complex, a truly rich tapestry. It can be seen through the history of the various Churches, or branches, or in the history of the individual countries, or through the changes in attitude and Christian doctrine throughout the last 2,000 years.

Through the unceasing effort of the early leaders and teachers, such as St Paul, the new faith of Christianity spread away from its original heartland, southwards through the northern lands of Africa, northwards into Asia Minor, eastwards towards Persia, and over the seas directly to Rome, which was the major power in those days.

Christianity began to adapt itself to the different beliefs and understandings of the countries where it spread. Its survival as a cohesive faith was due to the organization of bishops, who developed the notion of universality – that anywhere that Christianity spread the same apostolic message was to be taught.

Yet for the first 300 years there was much persecution, particularly in the Roman Empire, because of the refusal of the Christians to abandon their beliefs and worship the Emperor, who was considered by the Romans to be divine. But in 313 CE the Emperor Constantine (c.285–337 CE), declared that Christianity should be tolerated. It began to spread through all the 'barbarian' lands under the Roman aegis. Before his death, Constantine moved the focal capital of his empire to Byzantium and built the city of Constantinople.

Within 60 years, however, the empire had become permanently split into a Western empire based in Rome, and an Eastern one based in Constantinople. The Roman Empire fragmented as outlying provinces fell to barbarians. Rome itself was sacked by Goths in 410 and Vandals in 455. By 476 the Western empire was over and the European countries began to take shape, all with Christianity at the centre. In the

East, the Byzantine Emperor in Constantinople presided over what was to become the Eastern Orthodox Church, also known, variously, as Greek Orthodox, Russian Orthodox, Holy Orthodox. This Church shares a different culture and ethos from that derived by the West. It has its own proper tradition that stems directly from those earliest years. Eastern Christianity spread from Greece and Asia Minor, then northwards through the Eastern European countries into Russia.

It was in the Eastern Church that the first of the three great schisms within Christianity occurred. The Greek-speaking Churches excommunicated the Coptic and Syrian (Oriental) Churches in the fifth century because the latter did not recognize Christ as being equal to the Father, nor was he God perfected in man. That this church has survived to the present day is nothing short of extraordinary, given the centuries of persecution and minority status. But pockets remain in Egypt (Coptic), Ethiopia, Armenia, Lebanon (Maronite) and India.

The major split between the Latin and Byzantine Churches, called the 'Great Schism', occurred finally in 1054 CE. It had been brewing for a while. It was partly political (the natural antagonism between two great powers levering for superiority), partly the rejection by the Byzantine Church of the papal authority of Rome and partly doctrinal. The Byzantine Church rejected the Latin version of the Nicene Creed, in which the Holy Spirit is said to proceed 'from the Son' as well as from the Father. This became known as the Filioque clause, and proved to be, on the face of it, the insurmountable difference. There were other cultural differences, such as the basic organization of the institution. The Latin Church believed, and still believes, in one governing authority, the Pope, while the Eastern Church believes in a federation or a family or self-governing (autocephalous) bodies. Also the East believed the Christian Church was a community in which there were individuals, rather than a getting together of individuals who make up a community, as it is viewed by the West. The root cause of the Great Schism lies in the culture and psyche of those early practitioners. The Eastern church is less concerned with absolute doctrine than it is with tradition and state of mind. The emphasis is on mystery, the mystery of God in the Eucharist, the mystery of the Holy Spirit, the mystery of Christ as represented in the only too human icons. There is an understanding that man, by aiming for union with God, will, by the right means, find that he is changed by God dwelling in him. Today it is the Church in Russia that can best lay claim to being the heirs of the early Byzantine church. The fact that it survived Communism is a thorough testament to its unity and the depth of belief of the people.

After the Great Schism the Western Church became known principally as the Roman Catholic Church, and it is probably the largest of the Christian groupings. Its head is the Bishop of Rome, the supreme pontiff, the Pope, who is considered to be the Vicar of Christ on earth, and whose utterances are regarded as infallible. (Papal infallibility was affirmed as recently as 1870, by the First Vatican Council.) In its early years its one unifying factor was the adoption of Latin for all church use. This gave its adherents the feeling that they were part of a gigantic family, that it was genuinely a supranational Church, a being, almost, that had the highest of divine ordinance. It is not surprising, therefore, that Europe, from early times up until the late medieval era, took the name Christendom. (Many things, good and bad – such as the Crusades – were perpetrated in the name of Christendom.) Roman Catholicism has a great presence in developing countries and is often in the forefront of the struggles of oppressed peoples world-wide.

It was the desire not to be under the rule of Rome which was the primary cause of the Reformation, the third of the major schisms between the Christian Churches. It was an attempt to return to the roots of the teachings in the Bible, considered by many to have been lost in the top-heavy hierarchy of the Roman Church. The Bible was to be the arbiter of what was right, not the Pope. The German Reformation was started by Martin Luther's (1483–1546) *Theses*; while in Switzerland, Zwingli reformed the churches in Zurich, followed by John Calvin in Geneva. In Britain the actions of Henry VIII led to the establishment of the Church of England, part of the wider Protestant Reform movement. Another reason for this separation was the burgeoning need for the language of the churches to be in the vernacular, to cater specifically for local needs and cultures.

The Lutheran Church is represented in Germany and Scandinavia. Its central doctrine is justification by faith, not by good works. Calvinism, which influenced many of the Reform churches, including the Scottish Presbyterian Church, developed the doctrine of predestination. Calvinism in its various forms was highly influential in the early American colonies.

Protestantism in England became the Anglican Church. Today this is headed worldwide by the Archbishop of Canterbury. It uses elements of Catholic ministry in its hierarchy of bishops, priests and deacons, but the liturgy was simplified into a more Protestant mould by Archbishop Thomas Cranmer (1489–1556.) Anglicanism is inclusive. It is happy to embrace members from all ends of the spiritual spectrum, from Anglo-Catholics to Evangelicals.

CHRISTIANITY TODAY

The Reformation to a certain extent freed many Christians from the absolute need to belong to any of the established Churches. It threw up some extraordinary and charismatic people whose readings of the Bible gave them a slightly different slant on the Christian religion; this includes John Wesley, the founder of Methodism, George Fox, who started the Quaker movement and Joseph Smith, founder of the Mormons.

Christianity is spread throughout the globe. It is a faith with an enormous sense of mission as exemplified by all those who have carried the gospel throughout the last 20 centuries, and in those who take the gospel around the world today. In countries like Africa it is one of the fastest growing of all religions. Partly this has to do with the parallel African concept of the one creator God. The experience of their tribal cultures and of oppression, too, is crucial in how they interpret their Christianity – but it is none the less Christian.

There is probably no religion quite as diverse as Christianity. There are as many forms of it as there are countries. Does that make a mockery of the faith? The answer has to be no. All of them hold Jesus Christ at the centre of their profession, and if a Christian is defined as one who believes, fundamentally, in Christ, then that is what he or she is.

ISLAM

Islam is the third of the three great Semitic religions, after Judaism and Christianity. It is deeply rooted in the two earlier religions; on the most fundamental level all three share the same truth – that of belief in the one God. The meeting points between them are quite considerable. Even if they appear to differ radically in outward form, the intention behind the scriptures, the rituals and the doctrines is essentially the same: that of eventual union with God.

In one sense the history of Islam predates the birth and revelations of the Prophet Muhammad and goes back to the creation of Adam and Eve and the Garden of Eden. In the true meaning of Islam – that of 'Submission to God' – this is undoubtedly so. There is a direct correlation between the Bible and the Qur'an on the lives of the prophets. The Qur'an impresses that the prophets and good men such as Abraham, Isaac, Ishmael, Joseph, Moses, Noah, Lot, Jonah, John the Baptist and Jesus were all 'muslim' (meaning 'one who is devoted or faithful to God'), and submitted themselves to the true path of the one God.

God is the eternal essence, while man is capable of intuiting His essence through intelligence and will. A Muslim accepts that God is the prime mover, originator and overseer of everything – both in the physical and spiritual world. The first thing a Muslim learns is, 'There is no other God but God' – this is the essence of Muslim life and belief. God is supreme, He 'knows all and sees all'. Islam is a total way of life; there is no distinction between sacred and secular. Although there are two main forms of Islam, Sunni and Shi'a, it is nevertheless one of the most unified of all religions, regardless of country, race or colour.

The Prophet Muhammad and the Qur'an

The part of the world that cradled the birth of Islam during the seventh century CE was an area of great trading activity, a meeting place of cultures. It was also rife with stone-worshipping, polytheistic warmongering Arabic, and nomadic tribes with very strong interfamilial loyalties and little notion of a cohesive society. There was only one place that commanded any semblance of unity and was recognized universally as being holy, and that was the Ka'bah, the sacred house of Mecca, built by Abraham for the worship of the One God. But over the centuries people had strayed from this essential truth, and worship of the One God scarcely existed.

It was into this maelstrom of trading, warring and near-pagan worship that God chose to reveal himself again, to try and nudge his people back on to the right path, the true religion of Adam, Abraham, Moses and Jesus.

Muhammad was born around 570 CE in the city of Mecca, which was at the time a fairly prosperous trading centre. While he was young he travelled extensively with the caravans to trade with other countries, establishing a reputation for honesty and wisdom, which attracted the attention of a wealthy widow, Khadijah, 15 years his senior, whom he married when he was 25. In 610 Muhammad received the first of his revelations, which were, initially, largely met with hostility by those to whom he preached. It was his piety and unassuming modesty, coupled with his insistence and perseverance, which eventually gave power to his teachings.

During his first ten years of preaching in Mecca, Muhammad had many converts but he also made enemies – particularly among his own tribe, the Quraysh. They and others took a dim view of Muhammad's implied (and even stated) criticism of their way of life. His messages about the One God and the True Path hit at the heart of their traditions and he was regarded as a dangerous subversive – not least because he was seen to embody the life that he advocated. In 622, therefore, he fled to Medina with his companions (including Abu Bakr and 'Umar, both of whom were highly instrumental in the spread of Islam after the Prophet's death). The city's elders, weary of local squabbles and having heard of his teachings, had invited Muhammad and he was made welcome there. This flight is known as the Hijra, and 622 CE is the date that is taken as the start of Islam.

At Medina, the Prophet continued to reveal the Qur'an and Islam began to be honed into the religion it is today. But it was not only as a religion, a way of knowing God, that Islam was developing there: it was also becoming a social and political way of life. By 630 CE he had risen from being the religious leader of a small immigrant few to being the political leader of most of central and western Arabia – even Mecca had surrendered eventually. He died in 632 CE, a few months after declaring that he had completed his mission.

The Qur'an

The heart of Islam is the Qur'an, the holy book of Islam, revealed to the Prophet Muhammad in a series of visions. The Qur'an is regarded as the ultimate guide to the difference between right and wrong, good and evil, truth and error; and how a Muslim may discern the difference. One of the names of the Qur'an is El-Furqan, the Discernment. In the Qur'an are found not only the essentials of the Islamic faith, but also exactly how a Muslim should behave in all possible situations in everyday life. Written in Arabic, it is poetry of the most illuminating and inspirational kind. It contains all of the Prophet's divinely inspired revelations set out in 114 surahs, or chapters, which are arranged in order of length – the longer ones first, the shortest last – rather than in chronological sequence. The surahs from his earlier days at Mecca are more metaphysical in tone, and thematically they stress the oneness of God and His merciful nature as well as his creative power in the universe, His judgement at the end of time, and the origin, nature and destiny of man. 'He is God, besides whom there is no other deity. He knows the unknown and the manifest. He is the Compassionate, the Merciful' (Qur'an 59:22). Man's creation and the final day of reckoning are frequently mentioned together in the Qur'an as being inseparable parts of the whole of God's plan.

The Qur'an expresses the necessity to do good in this life, with the promise of the joys of the life hereafter in the Garden of Paradise. Doing evil will land you in Hell-fire — but man has a choice.

> By the soul and Him that moulded it and inspired it with knowledge of sin and piety: blessed shall be the man who has kept it pure, and ruined he that has corrupted it!
>
> Qur'an 91:7–10

Later, the teachings in the surahs from Medina begin to stress the application of the word of God in everyday life, with virtually no aspect of day-to-day practicalities overlooked.

THE FIVE PILLARS OF ISLAM

The divine messages that the Prophet received at Medina were distilled into the teachings (instructions) known as the five 'Pillars of Islam'. These are the five religious observances that every Muslim adheres to: the shahada (the profession of faith), salat (worship), zakat (alms-giving), sawm (fasting) and hajj (pilgrimage). Although these are prescribed in the Qur'an, they are not detailed. It was during the first three centuries after the Prophet's death that the full rituals were made clear, using a combination of the teachings of the Qur'an, the Hadith (verbal traditions), and the Sunnah (prophetic practices), both of which Muhammad gave to his companions. Muslims everywhere in the world conform to these five observances, making Islam the most unified of all religions.

The shahada, the profession of faith, is the underpinning essence of being a Muslim. It is not only the formula of the newly converted, but is repeated at every prayer and is recited with 'niyya' – true intention. 'La ilaha illa Allah: Muhammad rasul Allah', which means, 'There is no other God but God and Muhammad is His messenger.' The first part of this statement offers no quarrel with the creeds of either Judaism or Christianity: it is the second part which distinguishes it so absolutely because of its conviction that Muhammad is the last and greatest of all the prophets foretold, the Seal of the Prophets.

The salat is the daily prayer ritual to be performed five times a day, by oneself or in congregation. In Islam, because one's dialogue with God is personal and not through priestly intercession, it is no less an act of worship to pray alone than to pray in company. It is expected, however, that once a week, at least, praying should be done in company at the Friday noon assembly – al-juma – in the mosque. This is the public confirmation of a Muslim's membership of the community. Praying in the congregation enhances the feeling of otherness, the onset of the meditative state, and the feeling of being at peace and at one with Allah. All prayer is preceded by ritual ablutions, symbolizing purity. The ritual of the salat (worship) has three particular movements – standing, bowing and prostrating, each with its specific meaning and prayer, and is done facing the Ka'bah in Mecca. The salat is an act of inner cleansing, of reaffirmation of Submission to God, a request to be ever 'rightly guided'. The ritual formulae as laid down by Muhammad, the Hadith and the Qur'an, all combine by repetition to impress themselves on the psyche of the worshipper until the truth behind the words becomes a reality.

Islam is explicit in the matter of zakat (alms-giving) although no set amount is stipulated. Originally alms-giving was an act of piety, but it became an act of necessity after the Hijra, when the Prophet had to rely on charity as well as spiritual support. It is an act of pleasure to give some of what you have to those that have not, and it is not only the giving of material goods but that of time, skills and effort also are regarded as being part of the necessary duty of a Muslim who has more than he needs. Today, in some countries, the zakat is administered by agencies, in others it has been replaced by a Western system of taxation and welfare, with alms-giving reduced to a local level only.

Sawm (fasting) is the fourth pillar of Islam. To fast is to purify the body, heart and mind. During Ramadan, the ninth month of the Islamic year, all Muslims must fast for thirty days between the hours of sunrise and sunset. Not only must they neither eat nor drink, they must also abstain from sexual intercourse, and (these days) smoking. Also, anger, passion, gossip and slander should be avoided, thus contributing towards a total purification. The reading of the Qur'an (divided into 30 parts, one for each day) is regarded as necessary to the Muslim's attempt to touch God with the fast. The rules are relaxed at night and for those who are travelling, and for others who are unable to comply – but they must make it up as soon as they are able.

Hajj is the Great Pilgrimage, the fifth pillar. All adult Muslims, if they possibly can, must make a pilgrimage to Mecca at least once in their life. Arabic tribes, even before the birth of Muhammad, have always performed a ritual pilgrimage around the Ka'bah in what is now the Sacred Mosque in Mecca. The Ka'bah has special significance; it was given to Mecca by Abraham.

The Hajj is full of rituals that everybody follows, the most important of which is the wuquf, the standing ceremony on the plain of Arafat, which takes place on the seventh day of the Hajj, and lasts until sunset; during which time a leading imam preaches a sermon based on the Prophet's Farewell Sermon. It is a gathering of great joy and energy of up to one million people, all celebrating the numinosity of Allah. The following day there is a throwing of rocks at a post, symbolizing Abraham's repudiation of Satan, and the 'feast of the sacrifice' which commemorates the sacrifice Abraham made of a lamb in place of his son Isaac. This 'feast' is celebrated all over the Muslim world so that some of the joys of the Hajj may be experienced by everyone even if they are not at Mount Arafat. On returning to Mecca, the pilgrims kiss the Black Stone that is set into the Ka'bah. The Hajj is not only a spiritual exercise, the summit of Islamic worship, but is the strongest possible affirmation and expression of Islamic unity and joy.

There is another duty expressed in the Qur'an to which the Muslim should adhere, and that is the Jihad, or Holy War. Jihad derives from an Arabic word meaning to struggle or to strive. It refers as much to the battle of overcoming one's personal demons as it does to waging war against an external enemy. A Jihad is only called for when Muslims perceive a threat to their existence. The inner Jihad is another step on the path of purification in order to seek unity with God.

OTHER DUTIES AND SOCIAL INJUNCTIONS

Certain other injunctions towards right living are laid down in the Qur'an. The Muslim is forbidden to eat pork, to drink wine, to gamble, to be a moneylender, to be unethical in thought or deed. There are clear guidelines for marriage, divorce, inheritance, the treatment of women and slaves, codes of dress and every aspect of social behaviour. Rights for women (with laws of inheritance and property in their favour, *and* the right for women to divorce their husbands) were enshrined in Islam over 1,300 years ago. There is no injunction in the Qur'an for the complete covering of the female form. It is simply expressed that both men and women should wear modest and unrevealing clothing.

FESTIVALS

The Muslim year moves backwards through the Gregorian solar calendar because it does not use leap years – in ten years, for instance, its New Year moves backwards four months. Muharram is the first month of the year, when the Hijra (Muhammad's departure from Mecca to Medina in 622 CE) is celebrated with the telling of stories about the prophet and his companions. The Birth of the Prophet falls on the twelfth day of the third month, the whole of which is dedicated to his memory. The longest festival is Ramadan, the month of disciplined fasting during daylight hours. Ramadan commemorates the revelation of the Qur'an to the Prophet on the Night of Power, Lailat al-Qadr. The end of Ramadan is 'Id Al-Fitr, End of the Month of Fasting, when the fast is not only broken by a feast but gifts are given to the poor and needy. The most important Muslim festival is the four-day 'Id Al-Adha, the Festival of Sacrifice – the feast at the end of the Hajj, commemorating the sacrifice of a sheep by Abraham. It is a time of remembering and of communion with God as well as celebration of the return from pilgrimage.

THE HISTORY OF ISLAM

On the Prophet's death in 632 CE Abu Bakr was elected leader. Islam continued to spread under the caliphates of Abu Bakr and 'Umar (634–44) – the Arabs now controlled Egypt, Palestine, Syria, Mesopotamia and Persia. During 'Umar's reign the essentials of the Shari'a law and the systems of Muslim government were laid down.

Then 'Umar was assassinated and the pious 'Uthman was chosen, mostly because he was malleable. Islamic expansion continued into Cyprus, Rhodes, the Anatolian coast and many Mediterranean ports. 'Uthman's best achievement was the 'recension' of the Qur'an – accurate copies made from the original text. 'Uthman was murdered in 656 and Ali (c.589 CE) was elected as successor. But he incurred the wrath of the Ummayad clan, and in particular the governor of Syria, Mu'awiyah, who raised an army. Ali compromised when he could have defeated Mu'awiyah. The seed was sown for Islam's great division into two sects, Sunni and Shi'a. Ali was murdered in 660 by the Kharijis, the 'seceders' who became the third major Islamic sect. The caliphate fell to his son, who was forced into a treaty – which the governor of Syria promptly broke. The minority Shi'a followed Hasan to Iraq. Mu'awiyah now commanded the allegiance of the majority, Sunni, and declared himself to be the Grand Caliph in Damascus. His success in 661 led to the foundation of Islam's first great dynasty, the Ummayad.

But in spite of internal wranglings, increasing obsession with acquisition of worldly wealth and acute self-preservation, the Islamic empire during the first century after the death of the Prophet expanded in the most phenomenal fashion. Under the Ummayads, the Arabs conquered Spain and in the East crossed the Indus into India.

Two hundred years after the death of the Prophet, the Islamic empire stretched from the Pyrenees in the West to what is now Bangladesh in the East. It was a time of enormous cultural flowering and cross-pollination with other civilizations, but effectively it was too large an empire to be held under one ruler alone. Politically Islam split, spiritually it remained united.

By the end of the fifteenth century, Christianity and the Crusades had dented Islamic rule in Palestine, and Spain had returned to Christian rule (with the assistance of the Spanish inquisition). Under the Ottoman Turk, Islam spread through Turkey, Eastern Europe and the southern Balkans and dominated the area for another four centuries. Under the Moguls, Islam spread through the Indian subcontinent. Islamic traders carried the Faith down the East African coast to Tanzania, through the Sahara to Nigeria, to Malaysia, Indonesia, China. Converts were many, as much by example as proselytizing, and they found themselves part of a vast, mostly united, Muslim family, regardless of race and origin.

As Islam spread and diverged the need for a standard law – the Shari'a – became apparent. To a great extent this law has defined and shaped Islam's empires, and interpreters of the Shari'a had (and still have) great social and political influence. The Sunni scrutinized the Hadith (the sayings of Muhammad and his companions) for help in interpreting uncertain points in the Qur'an. Thus the Shari'a – as used by the majority of Sunni – was based on the Qur'an, the Hadith, Sunna (practice) consensus of the community (ijma), with – if necessary – analogical reasoning. Five principal schools of Shari'a law (one of which is Shi'a) were accepted by the tenth century, and are still in force today. Each school places a slightly different emphasis on certain matters of doctrine and theology.

The Shi'a believe that Ali was the first imam, and, over the centuries, have developed their own legal framework and theology. They do not subscribe to ijma, but believe in the authority of their scholars and the infallibility of the imams, who, as ayatollahs, are filling the office of the imam until such time as al-Mahdi should return. The Shi'a are significant in Iran, Iraq, Pakistan, parts of India, Turkey, Lebanon, and Syria.

There are other sects, such as the Ismailis who follow much the same path as the Shi'a; the difference lies in believing that Isma'il, in the eighth century, should have become the seventh imam. Most of the Ismailis are now divided into two branches, the Musta'lis in Bombay and the Nizaris, led by the Aga Khan. Smaller offshoots are the Nusayris and the Druzes.

There is one particular path of Islam that has shone throughout the centuries, in spite of persecution, and this is Sufism. The Sufis follow the esoteric path of Islam, but not necessarily by withdrawing from the world. There were always ascetics and mystics, but the Sufis rose as a potent force at the time of the Sunni/Shi'a split. Their spirituality was a reaction to the greedy acquisitiveness of the caliphs, who were paying lip-service only to the Islamic ideal.

The Sufis have produced some of the world's most remarkable scholars, philosophers and writers, who were often at odds with the pious mainstream: such as al-Hallaj, whose utterance, while in a transcendent state, of 'I am al-Haqq' ('I am the Real'), caused his execution. The theologian-philosopher Al-Ghazali was perhaps the most instrumental in drawing together some of the disparate threads of Sufism and orthodox Islam. He expressed the importance of the inner life without denying the necessity of the law and the worth of philosophy. Essentially it was to put God at the centre of all things: this is the central tenet of Islam, but the orthodox suspected Sufi methods – instead of using the mainstream schools, Sufis passed the teachings on from master (shaykh) to pupil in communities or schools of their own. These separate schools grew into the many different Sufi orders, several of which are still practising in many parts of the world.

ISLAM TODAY

Every culture or empire has its cycles and Islam is not exempt. For centuries, Islam was in the vanguard of scientific discovery, cultural ideas and philosophical thought. But from the time of the European Renaissance Islam's primacy in all these areas began to be eroded. The decline of the Islamic Ottoman Empire started in 1683 when it failed to take Vienna and eventually lost the Balkans to the Austro–Hungarian

Empire. In other Islamic areas – India, Indonesia, North Africa – the newly powerful European countries such as Britain, France and Holland dominated through trade and rule during the eighteenth and nineteenth centuries. By the twentieth century even some of the heartlands of Muhammad and the smaller Gulf States were virtually under British and French governance. The glorious empire of Islam was almost completely subsumed by the West.

The concept of pan-Islamic agreement was put forward in the nineteenth century, in an attempt to counteract the already perceived threat of Western materialism. But because the diversity of the Muslim countries made a pan-Islam cohesiveness impossible, it was swiftly followed by pan-Arabism. This was rejected as likely to breed colonialism. Yet the idea of Islamic nationhood was growing (particularly with increasing contact with individual Western nations). This and the need for the Indian subcontinent to free itself from Arab imperialism were the forces behind the birth of the Islamic state of Pakistan.

Islam has never been a static religion. Its philosophers, thinkers and intellectuals throughout the centuries have applied its ethics to their own and changing times. But the dilemma for Islamic countries of how to deal with the encroachment of Western technology, values and influence still has not been entirely resolved. The assimilation of technology is not a problem, given that science was always part of Islamic culture. It is the values and influences that come with it which threaten the fabric of Islam – many Muslims feel that their way of life, their Islamic centre, is being deeply eroded by Western modernization.

Now there are fundamentalist movements seeking to return Muslim countries to Islam, calling for a complete application of Shari'a law (even in countries where civil law is also applied) and a more literal interpretation of the Qur'an. Their aim is a deep commitment to the true roots of Islam and love of God while bringing themselves into the modern world on their own terms.

BAHÁ'Í FAITH

The Bahá'í faith is the most recent of all world religions. The whole ethos of the Bahá'í Faith is Unity. The ultimate goal is that all peoples of the world, of whatever race, creed and other differences, should live in harmony, both in the religious sense and in the political, temporal and spiritual worlds. It propounds the commonsense as well as the devotional. To a certain extent it is religion pared down to a few essential beliefs and to the minimum of observances.

> You are the fruit of one tree and the leaves of one branch.
>
> Baha'u'llah

BAHA'U'LLAH

Baha'u'llah, which means 'Glory to God', is the founder of the Bahá'í faith. He was a man of deep integrity and had a profound influence on all those who met him. He was born into a respected and respectable family in 1817 in Tehran. He was destined to follow in his father's footsteps as a government official, but he always had an inclination towards the spiritual. He became part of an extreme Shi'ite sect, whose leader was Said Ali Muhammad (1819–50), known as the Bab, or the Gate. The Bab pronounced himself as the prophet to foretell the coming of the twelfth Imam, the lost Imam of Shi'ite orthodox teachings, who would head the New World Order, and presage a new coming of age in religion. The underlying theme of this offshoot of orthodox Shia Islam was of turning the adherent towards an inner truth. This inner truth would supersede the external Islamic laws. The Bab wrote extensively and with a certain sense of militancy and duty, urging followers to seek the inner truth. There was an expectation worldwide of the imminent appearance of a new Messiah.

The Bab was persecuted and imprisoned, as were many of his followers. He continued to write and his movement continued to survive, even if it did not flourish. It became increasingly militant, more concerned with imposition and forced change rather than with the far slower process of listening to the Inner Truth. This led to uprisings followed by repressive violence from the state during the year 1848–51, in which between 3,000 and 4,000 adherents of the Bab were killed.

The Bab was executed in 1850 and two years later, following an attempted regicide of the Shah, many Babis were either imprisoned in the notorious Black Pit dungeon of Tehran or executed. It was in the Black Pit, and facing the possibility of execution, that Baha'u'llah received his direct Revelation from God. It came in a dream and told him that he should not be afraid, nor regret anything that had happened so far, because his life and words would render him victorious. Shortly afterwards Baha'u'llah and other Babi adherents were exiled to Baghdad.

Here he refined the message of the Bab, relieving it of its militancy and replacing it with obedience to the state. Man should turn inward for his salvation, not outward to wars and brutality. Over the next ten years Baha'u'llah gained a substantial following. This alarmed the authorities.

Although Baha'u'llah had organized the disparate community of Babis, and had gathered many more disciples through his teachings and example, he had not during these ten years spoken of the Revelation he had received in the dungeon of the Black Pit. In 1863, most of the community in Baghdad was exiled to Constantinople.

In the twelve days before he left, Baha'u'llah had spent his time in a garden which he christened Ridvan (pronounced Riswan), meaning 'Paradise' in Persian. Here he gathered his community together and, before they left for their exile under the aegis of the Ottoman Empire, he told them that he was, indeed, the One of whom the Bab had foretold – the Promised One. This was the start of the Baha'i faith – although the seeds had been sown 20 years before.

After a short time in Constantinople he was removed to Adrianople (modern Edirne on the Western borders of

Turkey), but even that was considered too close and too inflammatory for the Ottoman government. He was then moved to Palestine to the fortress of Akka or Acre and was incarcerated there for over two years. His imprisonment did not stop hundreds of followers from trying to visit him, but they were turned away. After the death of a son he received permission to live under house arrest, but still within the prison walls. Here visitors and disciples and adherents were allowed to visit. After many years he was allowed outside to live at Bahji, where he was surrounded by many of his followers who regarded him with the reverence due to the Messenger of God. He continued to write, particularly on laws and ordinances, and was visited by many. After a total of twenty-four years of exile in Palestine he died on 29 May 1892.

THE BAHÁ'Í SCRIPTURES

Bahá'ís have an advantage over other faiths in that Baha'u'llah lived in an age when writing was the main form of communication – and he was a prolific writer. However, all Baha'u'llah's words stem from his own pen and therefore are not and cannot be adulterated. He wrote voluminously and often personally, although his precepts are universal. He commented widely on topics ranging from the religious and spiritual through to the arts and science to jurisprudence and social organization.

His most famous writing is the central book of the Bahá'ís: the Kitab-i-Aqdas (Most Holy Book) where Baha'u'llah outlines all the laws and commandments the Bahá'í is expected to follow. He also wrote Kalimat-i-Maknunih (Hidden Words) which contains 153 proverbs on the nature of universal religion and the truths which underlie all manner of things. In Haft-Vadi (Seven Valleys) he describes the various stages of mysticism: the Valleys of Search, of Love, of Knowledge, of Unity, of Contentment, of Wonderment, and of True Poverty and Absolute Nothingness. Other titles include Glad Tidings, Words of Paradise, Book of the Covenant, Four Valleys and the Book of Certitude.

There are also scriptures by the Bab, the forerunner of Baha'u'llah, and also commentaries and treatises on these scriptures by Abdul-Baha. The majority of these scriptures remain in manuscript and have been seen by very few.

Those of the scriptures that are available for everyone to read are by Shoghi Effendi, a disciple and convert, who wrote mainly in English, rather than Arabic or Persian. Baha'u'llah, on the other hand, wrote directly and simply in Persian or in Arabic. But the Bahá'í takes his words on trust – as does any adherent to a religion – and finds divine inspiration in them, with their central themes of tolerance, understanding, goodness, unity, obedience to God's will.

BAHÁ'Í BELIEFS AND PRACTICES

The Bahá'í faith upholds the unity of God, recognizes the unity of His Prophets, and inculcates the principle of the oneness and wholeness of the entire human race.

Shoghi Effendi, Guidance for Today and Tomorrow

The Bahá'í believe in the one God and in his Messenger, Baha'u'llah. Baha'u'llah is the latest in a long line of messengers sent by God to interpret His divine strictures according to the needs of the world of the time. Just as Moses was succeeded by Jesus Christ, who was succeeded by Muhammad, so Muhammad was followed by Baha'u'llah. It was God's intention that his Word should be spread again. The Bahá'ís call it Progressive Revelation. It is regarded as obvious that God's Word is universal and, although clothed in different forms, is common to all religions. What is different are the social issues. These change as the world changes and with each change a New Messenger is sent. He will lay down the guidelines for the new social order, sometimes abrogating old laws which have little pertinence, in favour of new ones which do.

Because we are all members of the human race, we are all one family, with obligations to each and every one. As far as the Bahá'í is concerned, there is no difference, or potentially there should be no difference. The Bahá'í is urged towards equality of race, religion, sex, status, occupation, language, etc. He believes in justice; only with true and impartial justice may the ills of the world begin to be solved. To arrive at true justice, the Bahá'í needs a conscience. Poverty and starvation are matters of conscience and must be tackled both individually and collectively. And there must be the will to do it. The way towards conscience, justice and equality is through education. This is fundamental. A quest for learning and understanding must be instilled into each and every one of us. Prejudice is eliminated through education, because prejudice is fear and knowledge will cut through fear. A Bahá'í is also concerned that religion and science should be complementary, not adversarial. It is the duty of every Bahá'í, as far as he or she is able, to improve the lot of those around him, to educate and to proselytize by example. Unshakeable faith, kindness, selflessness, love and being non-judgemental all point to a morality and example that is often unbeatable and awe-inspiring.

The Bahá'í consider that as the womb is the preparation and place of growth for a baby before it exits into the outside world, so this life is the preparation and growth for the hereafter. But the whole process of birth, life, death and afterlife are not taken as separate incidents, but as different stages along the same path. What binds all the disparate elements is the soul, which came from God and will return to God.

Prayer and Meditation

Much emphasis is placed on prayer and meditation. Both are tools for self-discovery and enlightenment. They calm the nerves and still both external and internal turmoil. They induce a feeling of peace and at-one-ness. Prayer is the channel between the individual and his Creator; meditation is about being in touch with the inner self. The importance of peace, harmony, discussion and tolerance is emphasized. There are five distinct stages in the process of prayer and meditation: prayer, meditation, inspiration, volition, action.

There is no ritual to speak of. What there is, is derived from the Islamic model. If one prays one should turn toward Haifa where the prophet is buried. The Bahá'í is enjoined to pray daily. He may do this in different ways, depending on personal or possibly cultural preference. He may use a form which may be said at any time of the day and which lasts about fifteen minutes. Or he may recite a shorter prayer three times a day: morning, noon and evening, or maybe use a very short one which is said daily around noon. Whichever is adopted, it is an integral part of the day; a constant reminder of who and where we are and an acknowledgement of God in all our doings.

FESTIVALS

The Bahá'í calendar was inaugurated by the Bab in 1844 and ratified by Baha'u'llah. There are 19 months each of 19 days, which makes 361 days in the year, so 4 days (5 in a leap year) are added between the eighteenth and nineteenth months. The years are divided into cycles of 19, called Vahids, and every nineteen cycles is a Kull-i-shay. The calendar follows the solar year and there are no moveable feasts. The most important festival is that of Ridvan, which takes place over 12 days at the end of April. This celebrates and commemorates the 'Declaration of His Mission to His Companions'.

Work is to cease on 9 days of the year: the first, ninth and twelfth days of Ridvan; the 5 anniversaries of the declaration of the Bab, of the birth of Baha'u'llah, the birth of the Bab, the ascension of Baha'u'llah, the martyrdom of the Bab; and at the feast of Naw Ruz (21 March, New Year). There is an obligation to fast for 19 days before Naw Ruz.

Other celebrations are the Day of the Covenant, Birth of Abdul-Baha and Ascension of Abdul-Baha. Apart from these, Bahá'ís get together at the beginning of every month for the Nineteen Day Feast, at which there are readings and prayers, and occasionally music. The idea is to generate the spirit of unity and sharing so important to Bahá'ís.

THE BAHÁ'Í FAITH TODAY

Following the death of Baha'u'llah, the mantle of leadership fell on the shoulders of his son, Abdul-Baha, who travelled to the West between 1911 and 1913, as a result of which the faith gained many new converts. At first many members were also Theosophists or Spiritualists or semi-adherents of other cultic movements, or even held affiliation with one of the established Churches. But the major consequence of Abdul-Baha's Western travels was that Western membership of the Bahá'í faith became exclusive. At about the same time, internal and factional disputes led to the principle that moral and social concerns took precedence over any occult and metaphysical one. The Bahá'í faith is nothing if not practical.

In his will, Abdul-Baha stipulated that there should always be an hereditary Guardian, who was to work with the as yet unestablished Universal House of Justice, as the leader of the community of Bahá'í. The first such Guardian, Shoghi Effendi Rabbani (1897–1957) was instrumental in laying down the precepts of both local and international organization that exist in the Bahá'í community today. He was ardent in his presentation of the faith and set about dynamic missionary work throughout the world. But his death left the community without a new Guardian, because he had nominated none. More than that, he had excommunicated all his male relatives, so that none could be found there. It seemed, in 1957, that the whole faith might be on the verge of collapse because one of the fundaments of Bahá'í was missing. It was proof of Shoghi Effendi's efficacy in organizing the basic administration that the first Universal House of Justice was elected, with little difficulty, by the National Assemblies.

These National Assemblies are the reason that the Bahá'í faith has managed to remain largely intact and unified, because there are no churches and there are no priests. The power of the clergy was something that Baha'u'llah deemed unnecessary and corrupting. He believed that the power of His word in an age of increasing literacy meant that people would be able to think for themselves rather than being dependent on the interpretations of the clergy, however scholarly and well-intentioned. He also believed that each member of the faith has a duty not only to promulgate but to enact the principles of Bahá'í in daily life, to be an example, precisely as he was. Their way of life should be reflected in what they do.

In the absence of any priesthood there are various elected bodies. At the top of these is the Universal House of Justice, based in the Bahá'í World Centre at Mount Carmel in Israel, for which an election is held every five years. This body is the supreme guide of the direction and progress of the faith. Under this international umbrella there are the national and local bodies. Elections for these are held every year. In accordance with the precepts laid down by Baha'u'llah, all disputes must take place with a willingness, not only to see the other point of view, but to resolve them.

> Nations and tribes of the world, who are always at war, turn your face towards unity and let the brightness of its light shine upon you.
>
> Baha'u'llah

Baha'u'llah envisaged a commonwealth of nations, with an international body which would settle disputes; a world with a common currency and a common system of weights and measures; a world with a common language – either a new one or an existing one. Of these (vitally important) measures only one has come to fruition, the United Nations. But the world's usual method for solving disputes is flawed, according to the Bahá'í, because it is done with antipathy and polarization instead of with sympathy and agreement.

The spread of the Bahá'í faith worldwide is quite considerable: there are perhaps two million adherents. It spreads by word of mouth, by others' observance of the life of a Bahá'í, and by missionary zeal. They promote themselves as an entirely separate and new tradition – even if its original derivation was from an Islamic sect. Some commentators feel that for all its self-promotion as a world faith, it is quite possible that it will undergo a schism or implode into small and negligible pockets. Others think that the Bahá'í have done good work and can rightly claim to be a global faith. The

Bahá'í have actively adapted their faith to a changing world – not by altering texts or beliefs but by rational organization, appealing to the needs of the times by making it conceptually attractive, and by looking to the future.

ZOROASTRIANISM

Around 2,000 years BCE a wave of nomadic tribesmen (known today as Indo-Iranians although they called themselves the noble ones, Aryas), passed through northern Persia en route for India, where they eventually absorbed the Indus Valley civilization. Some of these peoples, however, settled in lands on the way and took up an agricultural way of life. Their religion was based on their earlier nomadism; no temples or images and using fire as a ritual focus. It was simple, fatalistic, sacrificial and polytheistic. Their gods and devils were abstract forces, rather than representational, drawn either from nature (wind, rain) or from the nature of man; relating to concepts such as Truth or Lie, Victory or Procrastination. Sacrifices were made to please the gods and to ensure that the world continued on the path of asha, Truth. Priests held sway over ordinary people and were possibly even more powerful than kings, because they alone held the power of interpretation of the wishes of the gods.

Its creation, myth and cosmology reflected the wide-open geography of the area in which it was conceived. The spherical sky is made of stone, and resting in the water at the bottom is the earth, like a plate, in the centre of which is the original Plant, next to this the Bull and the First Man, Gayomart, and, stationary above all, the Sun, representing fire. Then the Plant, the Bull and Gayomart were sacrificed by the gods, and from the scattered Plant came all the other plants, and from the seed of the Bull and Gayomart came all other life. The earth grew mountains, the rains turned the water into seas and the sun circled the top of the mountain, introducing day and night. The sacrifices were a mythical representation of the offerings that used to be made to ensure the favour of the gods, the continuation of both the world and of asha, the eternal Truth of order and justice.

Into this relatively peaceful pastoral society, 500 years later, came a second wave of invading nomads, indulging in warfare, trailing new weapons and in general causing misery and injustice. Into this era of change and movement came the prophet Zoroaster.

ZOROASTER AND HIS TEACHINGS

Very little is know about Zoroaster. He is the material of legend and myth. Even when he lived is questionable: it was, until recently, thought to have been *c.*600 BCE. This is what the later priests, magi, of the religion decided. But as a result of scholarly delving into the scriptures, it is now acknowledged that Zoroaster probably lived at least six hundred years earlier. All that can be certain from scrutiny of the Avesta, the Zoroastrian scriptures, is that he was descended from the settlers of the first nomads, was an hereditary priest of the indigenous religion, and was married and had children.

He appears to have been thoughtful, spiritual and incensed by the unjust treatment of his peoples by the invaders. It caused him to meditate on the nature and origins of good and evil. He spent years in 'conversation' with God which led him to the divine revelation of his new faith, that of the one True God, Ahura Mazda. Eternal and Uncreated, the Wise Lord, Ahura Mazda, is wholly wise, good, beneficent and just, creator of all the spiritual and material worlds.

Being just, wise and all-seeing, Zoroaster's God, Ahura Mazda, can see into the hearts of and speak to everyone and anyone, not just the priests. Zoroaster taught that observance of God should be an intensely personal experience – such as his had been – with no need of priestly interpretation. Man and woman have a choice of responsibility, he says, between good and evil. Those who practise good will undoubtedly rise to heaven, those who prefer the path of bad deeds and thoughts will inevitably drop to hell; regardless of social position. In Zoroastrian teachings it is incumbent on every man and woman to live the life of right thoughts, right words and right deeds. Only thus will creation be cleansed of evil.

And evil does exist. It is not the creation of Ahura Mazda but of Angra Mainyu, the Evil Spirit, Uncreated but not Eternal.

Truly there are two primal spirits, twins renowned to be in conflict. In thought, word and deed they are two: the good and the bad.
Yasna 30.3

It is Angra Mainyu who curtails the all-powerfulness of the Wise Lord by constant opposition. It is Angra Mainyu who occupies hell and who created demons to wreak havoc on the creation of Ahura Mazda. So Ahura Mazda created the world and all its inhabitants as his allies in the fight against Evil.

To help him further, he also created the six Amesha Spentas, each of whom have a correspondence in the natural world: Vohu Mana (Good Intent and Cattle), Asha (Truth and Righteousness and Fire), Armaiti (Devotion and Earth), Kshathra (Dominion and Sky), Haurvatat (Wholeness and Water) and Ameretat (Immortality and Plants). His seventh creation was Spenta Mainyu, the Holy Spirit who, in effect, was the general of the forces. His correspondence is man, and therefore represents God in man, as epitomized by the priests who function at any rite. All these seven beings, also known as the Bounteous Immortals, were worshipped both as entities in their own right but also as aspects of God and as ideals to be aimed for.

In turn, the Amesha Spentas called on the help of the yazatas, who were the good, old gods. Angra Mainyu countered by using the daevas, ancient amoral demons, to attack the creation of good. According to Zoroastrian teachings, it was Angra Mainyu who killed the first Plant, the Bull and the Man. Evil triumphed – but for a short time only. The Amesha Spentas created life from death and brought the world, as we know it now, into being.

Angra Mainyu found he was trapped and condemned to spend his time in the cosmic battle between good and evil. Zoroastrian history tells that after the original death of the Plant, the Bull and the Man there would be 3,000 years of balance between the two forces. After 3,000 years Zoroaster was born and from that point, with the revelation of the Good Religion, it was acknowledged that evil eventually would be beaten and banished from the world.

This would not happen immediately but would take a further 3,000 years. There would be three more prophets (each born of a virgin impregnated by bathing in a lake which preserves the seed of the prophet), the last of which will rise from the dead to bring about the Final Judgement.

The soul of every man is judged immediately after death and crosses the Chinvat Bridge, which is shaped like a sword. If the dead person has been righteous and good, the soul, led by a beautiful woman, will cross the bridge on the flat side. If he has not been good, a verminous old hag will lead him over. But, as he crosses, the bridge will turn on its edge, and the soul topple to hell.

A final war between good and evil will rage. But the forces of good prove too much for Angra Mainyu. His strength is spent and he will be vanquished. The earth can now look forward to the 'renovation of creation' – Frashokereti. The earth does not die, it is not the end of the world – it is the beginning of the new era in which all may look forward to a life of goodness. It is one of the essences of Zoroastrianism that there is free will – the free will to choose between good and evil in one's life.

Early teachings suggest that after the Final Judgement (when body and soul are united) the wicked remain in hell for ever, but a later change in doctrine posits the idea that the wicked may be purified by a stream of molten metal and be allowed to take their rightful place on the new earth.

THE HISTORY OF ZOROASTRIANISM

Zoroaster preached for ten years with little luck. He took to wandering and eventually succeeded in converting a minor prince, Vishtasp. This was the catalyst for the Good Religion to spread through eastern and then western Iran, and into Medea. Cyrus the Great, first ruler of the Persian Empire, ordained it as the state religion and the influence of Zoroastrianism began to spread. It is certain that elements of the Jewish, Christian and Islamic faiths were influenced, and probably the religions of India, and therefore the Far East, too. The exiled Jews from Babylon, whom Cyrus set free, carried the notions of the Last Judgement and other eschatological matters back with them, which were incorporated into the Jewish doctrine.

Two hundred years after Cyrus, the advent of Alexander the Great and his Seleucid dynasty wiped out many of the priests to whom the oral tradition of the Good Religion was entrusted. Nothing had been written down, because writing was considered a foreign art and not suitable for sacred words. Much of the knowledge of the practices of the time are taken from Greek and Persian writings.

The Parthians, with Zoroastrianism again as the state religion, gradually expelled the Seleucids from Iran. They were the first to gather together the traditions of the faith. These writings were to form the basis of the Zoroastrian holy book, the Avesta. They were followed, after 400 years, by the Sassanians in 224 CE. During their rule of approximately 400 years, they put in place a whole ecclesiastical organization, with priests, magi, temples, rites, devotions. It was a Zoroastrian ideal, that state and church should be unified. But one of the consequences of his unification was that the power of the priests was as overweening as it had been before Zoroaster was born.

Nevertheless the Sassanians left a strong legacy of Zoroastrian writings. These were partially destroyed as the armies of the newest faith, Islam, became an occupying force. It took 300 years for Islam to dominate. In that time Zoroastrians were persecuted in spite of their prophet having received direct revelation from God (Jews and Christians were tolerated, on the other hand, and allowed to continue in their religions). They retreated into villages in the wilderness, where pockets of the Good Religion still exist in the Yazdi plain. It is amazing that the faith has survived in spite of 1,300 years of Islamic tyranny. It is estimated that there are 30,000 adherents still living in Iran.

During the tenth century, a band of Zoroastrians left for India – rather like the Pilgrim Fathers – to find a place of religious freedom. They became known as the Parsees (Persians). They have maintained a firm grip on the religion they brought with them and have risen to be one of the wealthier groups of Western Indian society. But because they were cut off from their roots, the faith also stayed static.

In the nineteenth century a Scottish missionary, J. Wilson, intent on converting the Bombay Parsees to Christianity, read in translation the Avesta, the scriptures, and the Pahlavi texts. He attacked the Parsees for the dualism he found in the scriptures and they were unable to refute anything, because there was no priest trained in the art of theological argument. The Avesta was used as a potent force in prayers, but no one could read it.

A priestly repetition of orthodox beliefs failed to satisfy, but two priests drew on mystical eastern beliefs in order to satisfy the need for a modern interpretation of Zoroaster's teachings. They found that he had intended fasting and self-denial (typical eastern mystical practices) as a way to God, and that reincarnation was implied. This was a total opposite to the Zoroastrian ideals of the family, of work, of living in the world to gain reward in the next – and yet many of the faith took refuge in it.

This was followed by further reforms, towards the concept of monotheism, encouraged by Victorian Western commentators. Theosophy introduced further changes towards the mystical and Zoroastrianism, at the end of the nineteenth century, had nothing with which to counter it.

By this time the Reform movement produced Gujarati translations of the Little Avesta, which meant that all Parsees could now read the sacred texts. But there was no one among them who could interpret and disseminate. The priests by now lacked all authority and respect, and their ignorance was castigated. There were factions and splits, and most of the old doctrine was lost under a welter of other, more argumentative, faiths.

It was not until the latter half of the twentieth century that Western interest in the original dualism provoked a corresponding interest in the Zoroastrian laity. There was a drive to unearth the more traditional myths and beliefs and reconcile them with the world as it is now.

THE DOCTRINE OF DUALISM

Dualism is the point which causes most dissent among commentators and scholars of Zoroastrianism. Some say that the Good Faith is essentially monotheistic, because that is what Zoroaster preached. Certainly he taught that there is One God. The confusion lies in 1) whether the Evil Spirit was primordial and therefore an equal of Ahura Mazda, or 2) whether the Evil Spirit's opposite and equal was the Holy Spirit, Spenta Mainyu (both of them lesser than Ahura Mazda). If Spenta Mainyu represents the good spirit of man, then Angra Mainyu is his dark side, man's evil intent.

The first notion is that of a cosmic dualism. Those that believe this consider that Angra Mainyu is the opposite of Ahura Mazda (because both were uncreated, i.e. always in existence), and thereby it implies an absolute cosmic dualism: that good and evil are equal primordial forces, constantly fighting one against the other. And also, because man is made in God's image, and because God is incapable of creating evil, man is not inherently wicked. Wickedness comes from the exterior forces of the power of evil in the shape of Angra Mainyu.

The second is an ethical dualism. This presupposes monotheism. The dualism resides in the life of man, in his moral choice between the two paths and in the battle between the two spirits, Spenta Mainyu and Angra Mainyu. Here evil is presumed to be the negative of good, a mental activity caused by man. Many say that this is the correct form of Zoroastrianism where the dualism is ethical, one where only God may create, his creations resolved into the two opposites of good and evil which are then manifest in the physical and mental worlds. In the Gathas, man owes allegiance to the Wise Lord and should fight evil ceaselessly, while recognizing his own capacity for ill.

The difficulty lies in the fact that no one really knows what Zoroaster preached. Undoubtedly he argued for faith in the one God. But did he, as the scriptures seem to state in some places, argue for the notion of cosmic dualism? Or was this something superimposed on Zoroaster's monotheism centuries later by the priests when they regained their power by becoming the medium of intercession between the ordinary man and the gods? The Parsees in India certainly *appear* to hold to a cosmic dualism, but whether this goes right back to Zoroaster, or only to the second century CE and the priests, no one can state for certain. The imposition of monotheism on what might be a truly dualist faith could be the result of the doctrinal attitudes of Western, particularly Christian, missionaries who first came across Zoroastrianism.

There is an agreement, however, between the differing schools of thought in two matters: man is a co-worker with God and that ultimately good will triumph over evil. In day-to-day application dualism comes down to a moral choice. Asha is the path to follow at all times, and man should avoid falling into falsehood, druj.

THE ZOROASTRIAN SCRIPTURES

No scriptures were written down until centuries after Zoroaster. When they finally came to be put on paper, it was in the language of Avestan, which was already dead by the first century CE. The oral tradition is supposed to have handed down the full Avesta, as received by the prophet during his revelations, but only 17 hymns (the Gathas) may be attributable. Some hymns (yashts) appear to be pre-Zoroaster, others are later – but even those are in Avestan.

The Parthians were the first to collate writings. The Sassanians consolidated. Then most of the Avesta was destroyed by successive invasions. What is left is a quarter of the whole, mostly liturgical and used in ceremonies.

What remains of the Avesta is divided into three parts: the Gathas, the hymns of Zoroaster, which are contained in the main liturgy, the Yasna; the yashts, sacrificial hymns addressed to various deities (a lapse into polytheism, or a collection of hymns from pre-Zoroaster); and the Vendidad or Videvdat – a law against the demons – which deals with ritual purity. It was first translated into Sanskrit in the twelfth century. The secondary scripture is the Zand – translations with commentaries, of which the sole survivor is in Pahlavi. In this Pahlavi translation, Ahura Mazda becomes Ohrmazd and Angra Mainyu, Ahriman. There are great difficulties for anyone who wishes to understand the scriptures, because of the obscurity of the languages and the ambiguity of the text itself – both of which lead to enormous differences in interpretation.

ZOROASTRIAN RITUAL

A Zoroastrian prays five times daily standing in the presence of fire. Because there were no temples until late in the development of the faith, worship took place either in the open air – on a hilltop, or by water – or by the household fire, and fire became the focus of purity. There are 'outer' ceremonies – where rites may be held in any clean place, and an 'inner' one, performed by purified priests and held only in an area of ritual in the fire-temple. Cleanliness is paramount – there is ritual purification before praying and although a birth is a time for rejoicing, in strict families the mother is still segregated for 40 days.

Men and women of the faith have equal access to the temples, and each may be initiated at the correct age. Initiation is an important family occasion, where the initiate bathes, drinks a cleansing drink and puts on the sacred shirt. In a simple ceremony he is handed his kusti, the sacred thread that goes three times round the waist and is knotted over his shirt. Initiation and marriage are the only occasions for congregational worship. Most praying is solitary. Such public priestly rites as there are, are either to please the Bounteous Immortals and the yazatas, to ensure that the world remains pure or to entreat for the fusion of the material and spiritual worlds – as will happen after the Final Judgement.

By far the most important ceremony takes place at death. The rites have a two — fold purpose: to isolate the impure body and to help the soul on its way over the Chinvat Bridge which is the gateway to the next life. There is a group of people, following a semi-segregated profession dealing with the bodies of the dead, who wrap the dead body in a cotton shroud and carry it on a bier (after prayers from the priest) to a stone tower. There the body is left to be picked clean by vultures. The soul is believed to linger for three days on earth, and therefore prayers are said during this time. The family and friends gather on the fourth day, before sun-up, to say goodbye with extra prayers and the promise of good deeds. Thereafter the departed is remembered monthly for the first year, then annually for the next thirty years. After that he is assumed to have joined the great company of all souls, and remembered yearly at the feast in their honour. (This does not sit happily with Zoroaster's doctrine of man's own accountability at Judgement Day.)

Zoroastrians celebrate many holy days, but seven of them are obligatory. These are the six gahambars and the No Ruz (New Year) day — to honour the six Amesha Spentas and Ahura Mazda. No Ruz day is dedicated to fire and looks forward to the triumph of good. Each festival lasts five days, and people visit temples, feast and give presents. There are also holidays when the names of the day and month coincide, which happens at least once a month.

ZOROASTRIANISM TODAY

Zoroastrianism has spread, albeit thinly, throughout the world. There are approximately some two million adherents worldwide. But one of the more surprising things about the diaspora is the similarity between the communities in India and those which have remained in Iran.

It is possible that the current followers of the faith are adhering to the rites and practices and beliefs that pertained in the tenth century, and it is possible, even probable, that the tenth-century practices were not those that were the foundation of the faith in earlier times. Zoroaster, after all, dispensed with priests. And the priests – an hereditary calling – disliked the removal of their power. Come the Sassanian empire they were in charge again, having revived old gods, old yazatas, almost translating Zoroastrianism into a polytheism of household gods and usurping power for themselves. This means that, to a greater extent, the practice of Zoroastrianism by the Parsees is as close as we can get to its practice in the times of the Sassanian empire rather than the original.

The question is, does it matter? Only to theologians and doctrine addicts. The main thrust of contemporary Zoroastrianism is a sense of happiness – man has not only to care for but enjoy the creations of God. This includes care of self, that a balance should be struck in all areas of life, a harmony achieved. There is no sense of man as a spiritual being hemmed in by the wicked material world, dying to be freed. The world is Good, and must be cared for. Everyone is responsible for his own destiny, has a duty to fight the cosmic battle, to ensure that the Good Religion is upheld by courage and integrity and to fight evil in all its places.

2 • THE RELIGIOUS LEGACY OF INDIA

HINDUISM

In the beginning the darkness covered the darkness, all that could be seen were indistinct shapes. Shut up in the emptiness, the One reached out to the Being and, through the power of that, was born.

First to develop was desire, which was the first seed of thought. Searching their souls, the Wise men found the seat of being in the non-being.

Rig-Veda 10:129

Thus, it is said, one of the major world faiths came into being. But where does Hinduism — as the West knows it — spring from? What and where are its roots?

Archaeological excavation in the Indus Valley has revealed a civilization that existed over 2000 years BCE. Found artefacts — some of which correspond to the eventual images of the Hindu pantheon — betray evidence of matriarchal, agricultural, peaceful and fertility-worshipping peoples who were overrun (c.1500 BCE) by the more aggressive, nomadic and patriarchal Aryans from the north-west. Hinduism grew out of the meeting of these two cultures — the warlike Aryans and the quieter farming Indus people, whose way of life was gradually absorbed by the invaders.

Their beliefs at that time were fairly simple. The Vedic Aryans essentially believed in good deeds (goodness was rewarded by heaven; but a bad life merited the eternal abyss), and the family. Worship at the time involved mainly hymn-singing and sacrifice. But as the Aryans spread south and east, and absorbed peoples in the central plains, the nature of the religion began to expand and change from the sacrificial element toward the theory of samsara (Sanskrit word for the eternal cycle of birth, death and rebirth) and the doctrine of moksha (liberation from samsara).

The acceptance of these two essential doctrines, along with the notion of karma – that every action has a reaction, or every deed has its opposite or complementary act – constitute the main thrust of modern Hinduism. It was around this time (1200 BCE) that these, and other concepts, were first recorded in the Vedas, the ancient Hindu scriptures.

After these doctrines began to be generally accepted, the ascetic hermits, known as the forest dwellers and wanderers, appeared. These sadhu or holy men, by the use of meditation, self-denial and self-flagellation, aimed to break free of samsara, often preaching a way to self-enlightenment that denied or contradicted the teachings of the holy priests, the Brahmins. These ascetics were the forerunners of Buddha and Mahavira (the founder of Jainism). It is from this period, around the sixth century BCE, that the Upanishads, the last books of the Vedas, are dated. This posed, for the first time, the theory of the one God; the individual soul, atman, in unity with the world soul, Brahman.

HINDU BELIEFS

A clue to the spiritual roots of Hinduism may be found in the Sanskrit names for Hinduism: sanatana dharma, the eternal religion, or vedic dharma, the religion of the Vedas. Sanatana dharma implies a faith that has always been, without beginning or end, into which all people may connect if they so wish, and which might be called by many names. The essence of the sanatana dharma lies in three fundamental concepts, on which all Hindus agree. They also consider that the concepts are common to all human beings in the world, whether the person is aware of them or not.

These three principal tenets may be expressed as:

(i) that everything in existence is an expression of God

(ii) that the proper aim of anyone's life is to come close, realize or merge with God

(iii) that worldly delights are temptations that divert the person from pursuing his true purpose of coming near to God.

Elaborating on these three concepts are the eternal truths contained in the Veda: God is everywhere and in all things, sentient and non-sentient; the soul, atman, is present in all beings, animals included; everyone goes through a constant cycle of birth, death and rebirth (samsara) until such time as samsara is broken and atman has achieved liberation (moksha), when atman merges with Brahman, the Supreme Spirit.

The sanatana dharma, the eternal truth, is the unchanging law of order, but there are more mundane dharma (duties) in the everyday life of a Hindu. The sadharana dharma is a general code of ethics, giving advice on pilgrimage, alms-giving, honouring priests, etc; the varnashrama dharma outlines the important, down-to-earth duties of a Hindu in his current life; but it is moksha that is the final aim of every follower of the Hindu faith.

To achieve moksha it is necessary to have knowledge, because only knowledge can drive through maya, the state of illusion which tricks us and holds us prisoner in the world of the senses, hiding the One behind a veil. To help penetrate that veil of maya there are four major paths to liberation or salvation in Hindu doctrine. Each is as valid as the other, with each meeting the different needs of the individual follower.

The easiest path for most Hindus, and the one which the majority chooses, is that of Bhakti (Devotion). By this Path, moksha is achieved through prayer and devotion to, and complete trust in, a personal deity (ishwara) as the representative of Brahman, the Supreme Spirit.

The Path of Good Works, or Karma (Right Actions), is used by those who have perhaps less time for devotional prayers, and seek moksha by the expression of good and the doing of good works, in all aspects of his everyday life. The person who follows this path conducts himself without any expectation of the personal benefits he might reap, using his talents for the betterment of society as a whole.

For the Jnana (Path of Knowledge), a teacher is required. It is an intellectual path, and release comes from study, immersion in, and understanding of, the scriptures.

The Path of Yoga involves the discipline of mind and body, bending both to the duty of praising god and of living correctly, eventually achieving liberation.

None of these paths is mutually exclusive. Indeed, many Hindus combine two or even all of them in their search for liberation. All four paths are commended to Arjuna by Krishna in the Bhagavad-Gita. Thus the ways in which moksha is attained are varied. The path to realization is not what is important, but the Supreme Spirit (Brahman) itself.

THE HINDU SCRIPTURES

The scriptures are fundamental to Hinduism. There are two forms, Shruti, which means 'heard' or 'God-given to man', and Smriti, which means 'remembered' or 'created by man'. Of the two, Shruti is the more important and includes both the four books of the Veda (in which are contained the beliefs and customs of what eventually became Hinduism), and the Upanishads. The Smriti texts include the Vedanga, and the great epics, loved and revered by all Hindus (and by many non-Hindu Indians), such as the Ramayana and the Mahabharata.

The earliest Shruti text, the Rig-Veda (hymns of praise to the gods and the forces of nature), stems from the Vedic period of early Aryan development, after they were well settled throughout the north of the Indian subcontinent. All the four Vedas were composed before the fifth century BCE. Some may have been as early as 1200 BCE, although not written down until much later. It took the great scholar Vedavyasa to rearrange the Veda into its four samhitas, or collections – the Rig-Veda, the Yajur-Veda, the Sama-Veda and the Atharva-Veda.

The Yajur-Veda is the 'sacrificial handbook for priests'. There are two versions, the older one being 'dark' or obscure, and the later one being 'white', indicating clarity. The Sama-Veda contains chants, tunes and melodies for the sacrificial hymns, while the Atharva-Veda is full of spells, charms and magical formulae.

Each Veda contains four different types of composition: the Mantras, psalms of praise, which comprise most of the Veda and are its oldest parts: the Brahmanas, a prose manual of ritual and prayer specially for the guidance of priests: these two emphasize the performance of worship. They are followed by Aranyakas, the 'forest books', guidance for the sage and hermit; and the Upanishads, which are complete works of philosophy. These two are linked together in emphasizing the philosophy of devotion.

Although the emphasis changed quite considerably from the beginning to the end of these writings, all the quintessential beliefs that are part of Hinduism today may be found in the Vedas, particularly in the Upanishads. They were composed at the end (anta) of the Vedic period (c.500 BCE), and as such form the basis of Vedanta philosophy. They contain texts on the nature of the soul, the relationship between the mind, body and emotions, the different ways of moksha, methods of prayer and meditation and advice to students of all persuasions.

The Hindu Epics and Smriti Texts

Most of these Shruti texts were only available to the priest, or to the educated Sanskrit-speaking Hindu. The ordinary man had little hope of understanding the central philosophies of his religion. But the thirst for information, for knowledge, gave rise to the Smriti texts. There is a vast amount of writing in all the Indian languages, which disseminates, discusses and explains the principles in the Veda, making it more accessible to the ordinary person. But the most important Smriti writings by far to the ordinary person are the two great Epics – the Mahabharata and the Ramayana.

The Mahabharata – 'The Great Epic of the Bharatas', Bharat being the ancient Sanskrit name for India – is a wonderful tale based on early legends, with over 90,000 verses containing various moral stories interwoven round the central one. It is probably the work of many authors, over a period of 800 years up to 400 CE, during which time there was much change and upheaval.

The sixth book of the Mahabharata contains the Bhagavad-Gita – The Song of the Lord. This is one of India's favourite religious poems – about Krishna's advice to Arjuna, one of the Pandu princes, on the subjects of morality, religious and philosophical values, the relationship between man and God. It is a very comprehensive exposition on all the many and various aspects of Hinduism, but at the same time making the faith alive to the ordinary Hindu.

The other great epic of Sanskrit literature, and another favourite for the same reasons, is the Ramayana, which also occurs as a Buddhist tale. Its rousing story of great deeds done by good versus evil, highlights the moral ideal of the obedient son, loving husband, dutiful king, caring brother, courageous soldier – all in the character of Rama. The dutiful and loving wife is personified in the character of Sita. Loyal friendship and service are epitomized in the form of Hanuman.

All the stories, epics and poetry embrace the totality of Hinduism, from the highly intellectual to the most feeling, underlining the essential points of the Hindu faith. They show how the Hindu should live his life in the right manner and to the fullest extent, for the good of all.

The later scriptures are all Smriti texts, compiled as accessible commentaries of the Shruti texts. These include the books of the Dharma Shastra and the Puranas. The Dharma Shastra (the Books of the Law) means, literally, 'the science of a code of conduct'. They indicate the 'rules' laid down for the different classes (varna) at the various stages in life (ashrama) – the essence of the daily life and worship of a Hindu. The most important law book, that of Manu, emphasizes (as in the Bhagavad-Gita), the importance of the difference in class; that each be defined according to its talents and abilities.

The Puranas are ancient stories and myths, composed between the sixth and sixteenth centuries CE, of which there are eighteen principal Puranas, six each dedicated to the exaltation, respectively, of Brahma, Vishnu and Shiva. They convey, through the medium of storytelling (along with the Epics and the Law Books), a more practical and accessible aspect of Hinduism.

THE HINDU PANTHEON

Ekam sat vipra bahuda vadanti.
Truth is one; wise men call it by different names.

From the Rig-Veda

The holy Hindu scriptures, the Veda, propound the idea of 33 principal deities in the earlier Hindu pantheon. Because of a mistranslation this has sometimes been interpreted as 330 million – the word for 'types or kinds' and the word for ten million (crore) are the same. This, naturally, has led to accusations of rampant pantheism when it really means that the One God had 33 distinct aspects, all with separate images and functions.

But the Hindu concept of God took some time to mature; over several centuries in fact, from the beginnings of the Rig-Veda in 1200 BCE to the completion of the earliest Puranas at the end of the seventh century CE. The earliest records are hymns of praise to the Gods of Nature, originally worshipped as separate entities, until eventually Vedic scholars pronounced them as different aspects of the 'truth', the one Supreme Spirit. The Upanishads (sixth century CE) first posited the idea of the one Supreme Spirit, which is called Brahman, and which is without form (akara) or quality (guna).

Because Brahman is without form and quality, it needs to be represented by its various aspects and images. It is known in the Hindu world principally through its three major aspects, the Trimurti. They are Brahma, the creative aspect of Brahman, Vishnu, the preserver aspect, and Shiva, the destroyer aspect, who is also God of fertility and regeneration. Their origins are in the Veda whence Prajapati became Brahma, one of the Adityas (Lords of Light) became Vishnu, and the Vedic Rudra (Storm God) combined with a pre-Hindu male deity to become Shiva. Two other figures, dear to a Hindu's heart because of the scriptures, are Rama and Krishna, considered to be avatars (incarnations) of Vishnu.

Their respective female counterparts are Saraswati, Goddess of the Arts and Learning, Laxmi, Goddess of Good Fortune and Parvati, who is worshipped in two forms. In her benign form she is worshipped as Shakti, the Mother Goddess, and in her terrible and destructive form she is Durga, or Kali, demanding blood-sacrifices. These two, Shakti and Kali, represent the dualistic play of cosmic forces – creation and destruction – within the One.

Other major gods are the elephant-headed Ganesha, the first 'son' of Parvati and Shiva. He removes obstacles and is prayed to before important undertakings. The second 'son' is Subrahmanya, who, as Karttikeya, is most popular in the south of India. Hanuman (He of the Large Jaws) is also revered, representing physical culture. He is the monkey god, Rama's general in the epic 'Ramayana'.

Some minor gods are still worshipped, such as Savita, the Sun God, and Agni, the Fire God, but in a small way. Most of the original thirty-three original gods of the Rig-Veda have slipped into the background, or changed names, perhaps to be worshipped locally, as village gods. And yet, if you ask a villager, Who is God? he will invariably answer 'Brahman', the One and Only. The village god and one's personal god (ishwara) are viewed both as separate entities, and as part of the One. Thus it is the principle of unity that endures.

And yet, another paradox: the Hindu religion places much emphasis on the images of God. Image-worship arose because it was easier for an ordinary person to worship a tangible image representing the divine concept of God. It was supposed to be difficult for the ordinary person to pray to a god without form or quality. But praying to the image is not worship of that particular object, it is an aid to the worship of god through concentrating on the image of that particular Deity. It is the accepted, even preferred, way of devoting one's prayers to god, as Krishna explains to Arjuna in the Bhagavad-Gita.

> The Supreme Personality of Godhead said: those who fix their minds on my personal form and are always engaged in worshipping Me with great and transcendental faith are considered by Me to be most perfect.
>
> Bhagavad-Gita 12.ii

But Brahman may be imagined in any form the worshipper cares to choose, and whatever form is chosen, it is still the One, the Supreme Spirit, to whom prayers are directed in the end.

HINDU BELIEFS AND RITUALS IN DAILY LIFE

The scriptures state that every individual has many component parts. There is the physical body, the senses, the emotions, the mind, the intelligence, an inner self (jeevatma) and the eternal self, the soul (atman).

> Atman, the spirit of vision, is never born and never dies. Before him there was nothing, and he is ONE for evermore. Never-born and eternal, beyond times gone or to come, he does not die when the body dies.
>
> Katha Upanishad

Atman is the one element that remains constant, while all else is subject to death, change and transformation. Jeevatma is the one exception, which can be construed as something like the personality. Jeevatma retains some sort of memory in the travel between the lives and it is to the jeevatma that Hindus refer when they talk about the transmigration of souls. Karma, one's actions and reactions, determine largely how the next life is going to start, and who you are going to be. By your actions through that life you will determine how close you are to moksha, or at the least to the promise of a better life the next time round.

Bound up with this are the basic concepts of Hindu morality: the four main reasons for all human actions. Dharma, to do what is right according to religious and moral principles, one's age, education, occupation and social division; Artha, to acquire wealth and possessions for the betterment of your family; Kama, to enjoy the physical pleasures of life; Moksha, to aim for liberation from the endless cycle of samsara, and achieve oneness with the Supreme Being.

As the Hindu goes through life, these four principles apply in varying degrees as varnashrama dharma. Varna is the class into which one is born, and each of the four classes demand their own particular kind of conduct and morality. Ashrama are the stages of life, also demanding particular ways of being in the world. Dharma means the religious conduct and duty that applies to each.

So to a great extent, it is the Hindu way of life that is important, rather than what he believes. There are certain key ceremonies and rites throughout a Hindu's life that are fundamental even if one does not worship in the general way. Apart from the various birth ceremonies, the first major one is the initiation of the sacred thread – open to the top three varna only – which starts the man on his first stage (ashrama) of life, that of the celibate student. The next stage is marriage, and its attendant duties. At this stage, three of the four aims, dharma, artha, kama, are especially important. Marriage is also for the creation of sons, for sons help with the ancestral post-death rites, as well as doing their bit to fill the family coffers.

These conditions of the marriage vows having been fulfilled, the man may venture on the third stage, that of the 'forest dweller' or the hermit, followed by the fourth stage of the wandering ascetic or sannyasin (one who has renounced the world). In these two ashrama the man may concentrate on his dharma and on moksha, or liberation from samsara. In practice only a few men enter into the two final stages completely (even fewer stay on the path of the fourth stage, to become a holy man), although many retired men do often devote themselves to worship, having given much of their worldly goods away and eschewing the normal domestic comforts.

Most devout Hindus pray daily, up to five times a day, either at home or in the temple. The Hindu temple is considered to be the home of a god and worshippers visit it rather as they would drop in on a special friend, with gifts of flowers, incense or food. Worship is not necessary with every visit, but due deference, such as bowing, is. The priest attends to the image of the god, and performs the daily rituals. Worshippers will listen to the scriptures, chant the mantra of the name of the god and pray. At festivals and on other joyful occasions devotional hymns, bhajans, will be sung.

The Hindu faith is a devotional one, with the worshipper praying to the god of the family, or his personal god. The day starts with ritual cleansing and offerings (puja) to the god of the house. Worship usually consists of prayers to the Wise, those who wrote the texts, to the gods, to the spirits of nature, to ancestors, and a general worship of humankind. There is one prayer, however, the sacred Gayatri mantra from the Rig-Veda, which should be recited by all Hindus at sunrise, noon and sunset: 'Om. Oh terrestrial sphere. Oh sphere of space. Oh celestial sphere. Let us contemplate the splendour of the solar spirit, the divine creator. May he guide our minds.'

All Hindu rituals are intended to impress, in the mind of the worshipper, the long legacy of those who have gone before, as well as remind him not only of his place in the scheme of the universe, but also of the interconnectedness and oneness of all things.

Funeral rites are important in India. Occasionally the dead are buried, but cremation is more usual. It allows the soul to be released and rise to heaven. The body is washed, anointed with incense and wrapped in a cloth and laid down on the funeral pyre, in the open air. A son is vital – he lights the pyre and pours ghee and incense on to it – for the proper execution of the funeral rites which aid the soul to find its new body for the rekindling of the next life. Without these rites, ghosts may be expected to linger. Prayers are recited by a priest and everyone stays until the flames are gone. The ashes are sprinkled, in the river Ganges – karma is washed away by the sacred waters. After the funeral the relatives of the deceased are 'unclean' for ten days. Even when life returns to normal, sons are expected to give regular memorial offerings – Shraddha.

Festivals are incredibly important in the Hindu calendar. They are mostly colourful and exuberant times of getting together, of processions, of joy, of affirmation of life. The most important four festivals, which are observed around the world, are: Raksha Bandhan, Dashera, Diwali and Holi.

Raksha Bandhan, celebrated in July or August, is symbolized by a red tie with which a woman binds a brother, or a male friend as an adopted brother, in ties of affection and protection.

Dashera, meaning the 'tenth', comes in September/October, straight after the nine-day festival (Navaratri) for the Mother Goddess, and is a celebration of the exploits in the Ramayana – signifying the triumph of good over evil. There are processions and dances and presents are given. It is very much a time for forgiveness, the making up of quarrels and affirmations of friendship.

Diwali is celebrated in October, and is the most popular of all the festivals. The name means a garland of lights, referring to the lamps that stand in rows both inside and outside houses. Puja are made to Yama, Vishnu, and Laxmi over the five days, there is feasting, fireworks, and the exchange of gifts.

Holi is a spring festival, and coincides with the spring harvest. Bonfires are lit, and people throw red powders or coloured water over each other.

There are festivals to celebrate Ganesha, Hanuman, Prince Rama, Laxmi, Vishnu, Krishna, Parvati, Durga, Saraswati. Each region in India, each village almost, has its own festival peculiar to itself. Festivals are also a time for fasting as well as feasting. Fasting is important in the Hindu ethos, for the doing of it gains much religious merit.

PILGRIMAGE

As with most religions, pilgrimage is an important issue for the Hindu believer. There are many shrines and temples and even ordinary places of great merit. Water is particularly venerated. The Ganges and Jumna rivers, especially where they join together at Benares (Varanasi), are considered places of great holiness and regeneration. The Ganges occupies a most sacred place in Hindu history as it is considered to flow directly from the gods – its water therefore is of the most holy. Pilgrimage is undertaken for various reasons: to bathe, in order to be cleansed; to circumambulate, keeping the shrine on the right-hand side at all times – a visit to a shrine accords prestige; to make the ritual offerings to the dead, the Shraddha; to scatter ashes of the dearly departed; to atone for sin, to make amends for some wrongdoing; or for faith healing – some shrines are believed to have curative properties.

There are 24 major pilgrimage sites in India, of which the four located on the points of the compass are considered supreme. They are the Jagannath temple at Puri in Bengal; Rameshwaram right on the southernmost tip of India; Dwarkadheesh on the west coast; and Badrinath, 3,000 metres up in the Himalayas. By having to travel this far, Indians get a view of another, probably unknown part of their country. They endure great hardships on their journeys, carrying heavy loads, eating and drinking little, sleeping in discomfort. This is all part of the moral attunement and religious merit that a Hindu receives for his pilgrimage.

HINDU PHILOSOPHICAL SCHOOLS

As philosophical reasoning became the dominant part of the religion, the sacrificial elements of Hinduism began to die away, not least because of the rise of merchants who had little time to devote to sacrifice. If sacrifice were necessary, it was performed in an increasingly ritualistic fashion by the local priest, the Brahmin. The emphasis of Hinduism was turning toward devotion.

By the first century CE there were six different but not completely separate schools, known as Darshana or Salvation Philosophies, in place in India. They may be grouped, roughly, in pairs.

1 Nyaya (The School of Analysis). The Hindu school of Logic, paired with:

2 Vaisheskika (Individual Characteristics). Atomist in its outlook and almost atheistic. It has much in common with Jain philosophy.

3 Samkhya (The Count). Fundamentally atheistic and dualistic. This school taught that all matter is composed of three gunas, qualities, in varying degrees – virtue (sattva), passion (rajas) and dullness (tamas). Matter (prakti) and soul (purusha) are independent of each other, yet involved. Much of the Samkhya school has filtered through and is present in other schools. It is generally teamed with:

4 Yoga. In the West, in its broadest sense, spiritual discipline best sums it up. In the Hindu context it usually refers to the school of philosophy of Patanjali (second century BCE). Enlightenment is achieved by following the Eightfold Path, plus the physical exercises that are needed to discipline the body into long periods of immobility while meditating.

5 Mimamsa (Enquiry/Investigation, Scriptural Exegesis). This was originally a school to defend and explain Vedic authority, that the Vedas were eternal and written by God.

6 Vedanta (The End of the Vedas). This is really the Upanishads or the 'culmination' of the Vedas. The fundamental Veda text is the Brahma-Sutra, but the Upanishads and the Bhagavad-Gita are also of importance. In theory Vedanta is theology, but in practice it is the only 'live' Darshana, incorporating the other Darshana, which are now only adjuncts to Vedanta. At one point in Hindu history, Samkhya and Vedanta were the two rival schools.

There are two schools of Vedanta, Advaita (seventh to eighth century CE), established by Shankara (probably eighth century CE), and the medieval Vaishnava school (twelfth to thirteenth century CE), of which the most important interpreter was Ramanuja (1017–1137 or 1157). Shankara harmonized the different threads in the schools of philosophy into one system as far as possible. In order to reconcile the Samkhya dualist theory he predicated that life was illusion (maya) and therefore Monist (that reality is only of one kind).

About 400 years later Ramanuja emerged as the most influential thinker of the age. Ramanuja felt that Shankara's way of knowledge (jnana) theory stopped short of the possibility of true merging with the One, which can only be done by including devotion (bhakti) to God and by abandonment to God's grace, which ultimately will never be denied. Shankara held that creation was a 'sport' devised by an impersonal Absolute, whereas for Ramanuja creation was an expression of God's love.

HINDU SOCIETY

Hinduism is a faith full of everyday action and not just a system of beliefs and philosophies. Over the centuries, the Aryans intermarried with indigenous peoples and ceased to be nomadic. This new tribal society demanded a different order and certain divisions began to appear so that there would be stability in the social order. These divisions, varna, were the basis for the class distinctions that became a fundamental part of both Indian and Hindu society. The Brahmins hold these divisions to be of divine origin.

There are four varna. Brahmins: the priests, knowledgeable on ritual and sacrificial lore, who learned and taught the scriptures. Kshatriyas: the warriors and rulers, governors and defenders of the settlements. Vaishyas: the farmers, industrialists and merchants. Shudras: artisans and craftsmen. The Shudra class eventually subdivided into the class who carried out the dirtiest, most menial jobs – the refuse collectors, the tanners, the butchers. They were known as the outcastes. In some places – particularly the villages – they are still segregated.

Class (varna) is different from caste (jati) although people tend to use the terms interchangeably, but it is important not to confuse them. Class refers specifically to the above four divisions, while castes are subdivisions classified by trade and occupation within the classes. Originally – as laid down in the book of Manu – movement between the classes was permitted. But over the centuries, family and vested trade interests resulted in the caste rigidity that to some extent still persists.

There are five principles in the social manifestation of the caste system:

1 Pollution. A lower caste is considered polluting by a higher one.

2 Commensality – eating together, or not.

3 Endogamy. Marrying within one's caste, or if not, at least in the same economic bracket.

4 Hereditary occupation and

5 Economic interdependence.

In the cities, commensality is no longer practicable, and because the world is a much smaller place, hereditary occupations and economic interdependence are less important and more flexible than before. But in marriage (and elections), loyalty to one's caste and varna are still important, whether overt or not. Erosion of these divisions is a slow process – even though Untouchability was abolished by law in 1950 there is still prejudice.

MODERN HINDUISM

Today Hindus practise their faith very much in the same way as that they have done for several centuries, yet it is not a static faith. There have been times in the history of Hinduism that the religion seemed either about to atrophy, or be subsumed, or change to such an extent under outside influences that it would become unrecognizable. Over the last 150 years particularly it has grown and adapted and consumed other ideas. Its flexibility is a clue to its continued survival and growth. The advent of the English, especially, had many intellectual, educational and religious consequences. They arrived at a time when the religion was possibly at its most feeble. The enthusiasm of Western scholars and intellectuals had the effect of reviving Hindu interest in their own teachings and gave rise to several major influential Indian teachers and thinkers.

Ramakrishna Paramahamsa (1834–86), did much (through personal experience) to promote the idea that 'all religions are one'. One of his disciples, Narendranath Datta became Vivekenanda (1863–1902), who was the first Hindu to travel widely and receive Western acclaim. He established the Ramakrishna mission and influenced many Western Vedanta societies. He raised morale, and social conscience, but did not manage to change the character of Hinduism. He died young, burnt out at forty. Following his death there was a surge in nationalism, and a defending of the absolutes of the systems as laid down over the years.

But although this new Hinduism touched the intellectuals, it did not reach the average person. It was not until the arrival of Mohandas Karamchand Gandhi, 1869–1948, that the reforms touched the masses. Gandhi was a religious leader with a strong political sense; a reformer, anti-Untouchability, anti-caste, anti-ritual pollution. Regarded by some as an incarnation of Vishnu, he was in favour of a personal rather than an impersonal God. He was assassinated by an orthodox Hindu sect who hated his reforms. But many of his reforms live on and although the process of implementation is slow, it is none the less happening.

Hinduism is now a worldwide religion, with Hindus living in many other countries, and the active participation of the West in Vedanta societies. It is a faith that is always developing, changing, adapting, incorporating yet allowing itself to stay true to the sanatana dharma.

BUDDHISM

This is the Noble Path which leads to freedom from delusion. He who treads this Path will end his suffering. I have told you of this Path ever since I knew suffering and its cure.

The Dhammapada 274, 275

Possibly the best known of all the ancient Indian religions – and certainly the most practised in the West – Buddhist teachings are over 2,500 years old. It came into being in a time of social upheaval during the sixth century BCE, when the old ways were considered unsatisfactory and there was disillusion with the might, wealth and tyranny of the ruling powers. This was not a localized phenomenon, but was a general dissatisfaction spreading from Greece through (what is now) the Middle East all the way to China. It was the time of an enormous flowering of the spirit: Greek philosophers, Hebrew prophets, the rise of Zoroastrianism, the birth of Jainism in India, Lao Tzu and Confucius in China. It is perhaps hard to imagine today – in an age of instant communication – that there was such an extraordinary near-worldwide movement: as if each exponent was touched by the same spiritual thread.

Buddhism comes from the word *buddha*, which means enlightened, and although there is one historical Buddha, from which the faith derives, it is not a religion of revelation (as with Islam or Christianity), but a system of belief that has no beginning because it embodies the Truth – the Truth that has always been and always will be, regardless of whether anyone accepts it or teaches it or not. It is a faith of great depth and complexity and here, unfortunately, there is only room to scratch the surface.

At the heart of Buddhism are the Three Jewels: the Buddha, his teachings and the community of monks and nuns, the Sangha.

THE BUDDHA

There is much myth built around the life of Buddha. Simply: he was born into a wealthy ruling family, his father being the head of the Sakya of the Gotama clan, in a village called Lumbini now on the borders of India and Nepal. He was named Siddhartha, 'he who has reached his goal' (but was more frequently known as Gotama or Sakyamuni), and brought up in exclusive luxury. He married young and had a son, whom he called Rahula, which means 'chain' or 'bond'. At the age of 29, deeming there was more to life than all his trappings of luxury, he left to take up the life of an ascetic mendicant. This was, at the time, the proper path for anyone who yearned for a life of spiritual truth and understanding.

Gotama followed a few religious teachers but apparently gained very little, and decided to search alone for spiritual enlightenment. With five other wandering religious companions he followed a life of increasing austerity and rigour, without achieving his desired results. The turning point came when, having fasted almost to the point of death, he realized that this extreme asceticism was utterly pointless, and rejected it in favour of a life of faith and contemplation. His companions, disgusted at his decision, left him.

Alone, immersed in meditation on the mysteries of death and rebirth under the branches of a sacred fig tree at Bodh-Gaya, Gotama reached the state of perfect Enlightenment. First, his previous lives passed before him, then he understood the meaning (dhamma) of the whole cycle of death and rebirth (samsara), and finally the Four Noble Truths were revealed to him.

He had become the Buddha.

Gotama could have entered nibbana (Sanskrit – nirvana, a 'blowing out', or final liberation from existence) at once. Apparently he doubted that the truth could be transmitted to others, but was persuaded otherwise. This led to his first sermon, 'The Turning of the Wheel of Dhamma' (dhamma means universal law, truth or teaching), given near Benares to a company among which were his five former companions. Through his teaching he won many disciples who were as attracted by his mien as much as his message. They included not only those who were willing to follow his wandering, contemplative and missionary path, but also lay people who had no desire to take up that life, but who were willing to support and follow the precepts as far as they were able.

Gotama devoted his life to spreading the truth of dhamma and nibbana. He spent 44 years wandering the fertile Ganges basin, taking his message to everyone, regardless of caste, class or sex. He created a new community of itinerant monks, the Sangha, whose mission was to teach the dhamma – not only through words but by their lifestyle. These are the Three Jewels of Buddhism, its foundation – the Buddha himself, the doctrine he taught and the community of monks and nuns, the Sangha.

The Buddha died at Kusinara when he was about 80 years old. Buddhists see the earthly life of the Buddha not as an entity in itself, but as the culminating life in a series of lives – all of which operated under the laws of karma (see below) and dhamma. They also understand that the historical Buddha was one of a series of buddhas, some of whom are yet to come – notably the Future Buddha, Maitreya, whose imminent appearance is anticipated by many.

THE TEACHINGS OF THE BUDDHA

By looking to the Buddha and his teachings anyone has the possibility of attaining true knowledge. Life's goal is nibbana, that state that transcends the physical, even the spiritual. It is a state of nothing and everything, way beyond our limited capacity for comprehension and description.

The first step toward the goal of nibbana is an understanding of the Four Noble Truths, the precepts that the Buddha set forth to the community in his first sermon. But to realize fully these Four Noble Truths, there has to be an understanding, first, both of the operation of dhamma, the universal law, and of karma, the law of cause and effect. Second, the Truths can only be approached if one is in the correct state to receive them.

Dhamma is the law of the universe, under which everything is subject to flux, change and decay. Everything in the world is interconnected under the law, which relates not only to the moral law of karma but to the universe and its physical laws. And not only to that, because dhamma also applies to individual components; therefore it is illusory that man is a truly independent being. He is composed of a great many elements, not exclusive to him, such as the five senses, colours, sounds, emotion, reason, will, sex, hunger, death. All these elements rearrange themselves after death to form another individual ready for incarnation. In this there is no recognition, as in Hinduism, of an individual soul or self that passes from one body to another. All the separate dhammas combine in a new birth which inherits the karma of previous lives. Thus all dhammas are regulated by the law of karma.

Karma operates in all spheres, physical and spiritual, of human life. What you do, how you behave, how you react to conditions – good and bad – determine the conditions of your next life. It is anything but fatalistic. On the contrary, any person with the knowledge of karma means that he may create his own future. This understanding of karma and its processes is also the basis on which one performs dana and sila, two exercises vital for achieving the right state of mind in which to receive the Four Noble Truths.

Dana, giving, is not necessarily alms, although that is included, but is more often a religious gift to someone already committed to the Path, such as a member of the Sangha. The act is performed with joy, care and dedication, and the gift is received in the same spirit. 'The man of wisdom who did good, / The man of morals who gave gifts, / In this world and the next one too, / They will advance to happiness' (Udangavarda IX Shilavarga). Each act of giving elevates the giver, until he is in the right frame of mind to come to sila.

The first act in sila is to 'Take refuge in the Buddha, the dhamma and the Sangha' (Dhammapada: 190) – which are the Three Jewels. This is the basic commitment before going further to inhabit Buddhism in everyday life by accepting the Five Precepts. These 'Do as you would be done by' precepts enjoin the Buddhist: Not to kill, not to take what is not freely given, not to indulge in sensual pleasures, not to lie, not to touch intoxicants.

Dana and sila are best performed with full knowledge of personal responsibility (i.e. it's the intention that counts) in the realms of karma, which elevates the calibre of both actions. This leads to a corresponding revelation that the material world is not the answer: that a greater joy is to be found in leaving the world of the senses behind. It is in this state that one begins to be truly receptive to the teachings of the Buddha.

The Four Noble Truths and the Noble Eightfold path

> Of paths the Eightfold is the best; of truths the Noble Four are best; of mental states, detachment is the best; of human beings the illumined one is best.
>
> The Dhammapada: 273

The Four Noble Truths and the Eightfold Path are at the centre of the Buddha's teachings. Every Buddhist in the world adheres to these basic precepts. Beyond that there are major differences set in two distinct schools of Buddhist thought and teaching.

The Buddha taught in his Four Noble Truths that:

• This world is full of suffering because it is reaping the effects of past karma. There is also an understanding, somewhere in our inner being, that this world is neither solid nor satisfying enough to be completely fulfilling.

• The cause of all this suffering is desire – not only desire for the material earthly things with which we hope to fill the gap of fulfilment, but desire and longing of any sort. But material things cannot sustain our need and so we start to come to an understanding of the nature of change and loss.

• Suffering may be ended by knowing the Truth, by reaching nirvana, the ultimate escape, the ultimate happiness – except that nirvana is beyond even happiness and defies description.

• The way to find the Truth that will end all suffering is by following the Noble Eightfold Path.

The Noble Eightfold Path

- Right knowledge – a recognition of the Four Noble Truths.
- Right thought – to approach all things with an attitude of peace and goodwill, leaving behind all negative emotions including sensual desires.
- Right speech – always truthful, wise and conciliatory, never inflammatory.
- Right action – to live according to true moral precepts. Stealing, adultery and murder are totally forbidden.
- Right livelihood – to carry out an occupation which actively does not do harm to others.
- Right effort – always to promote good intentions and to stifle the bad, so that right thought is ever in the mind and action.
- Right mindfulness – an awareness and consideration of everything, and to not give in to any desires that surface.
- Right composure – or concentration which allows further progression on the path.

All these eight precepts fall into three categories, the Threefold Discipline: right speech, action and livelihood are concerned with vinaya (morality); effort, mindfulness and composure with dhyana (spiritual discipline and meditation); and right knowledge and right thought with prajna (insight). None of these injunctions promote either extreme asceticism nor the giving in to sensation. Taken as a whole it is a balanced, yet uncompromising, attitude to life. It is apposite that Buddhism is also known as The Middle Way.

THE SANGHA

The community of monks and nuns (although there are none now in Theravada Buddhism) has always been revered by Buddhists – for two particular reasons. First, they have decided on the difficult path of renunciation of the world in order to follow the path to salvation and such renunciation is worthy of veneration. Second, they keep the truth of

Buddhism alive in their practice, in the preservation of the Buddha's teachings. This was originally done through oral transmission, then through the writing and translation of the teachings. Their monasteries were centres of teaching and in some places were the only schools. It is this community of monks which is responsible for the spread, not only of Buddhism, but of whole streams of culture to ancient and far-off lands.

THE EARLY SCRIPTURES

The early Buddhist scriptures were – as with other traditions almost everywhere else in the world – transmitted orally. Gradually they were organized in three 'baskets', or sections – the Tipitaka (Tripitaka in Sanskrit). It was in Ceylon in the first century BCE that they were first committed to writing. This is the Pali Canon, which some regard as the only scriptures of Buddhism – the later writings being mere commentaries.

The Tipitaka, as its name suggests, is divided into three distinct sections. The Vinaya-pitaka, the Sutta-pitaka and the Abhidhamma-pitaka. The Vinaya-pitaka, the Basket of Discipline, deals with the orders and discipline of the Sangha. It is probably the oldest of the three. The Sutta-pitaka is mostly devoted to some of the Buddha's discourses, arranged in four or five nikayas (parts) which later became known as the agamas or traditions. This is the key Buddhist scripture on the techniques of psychological and spiritual mind-training in which the idea is to induce a permanently changed state of reality – that is, complete elimination of the notion of self. The 'map' of these psychological and spiritual states as presented in the Abhidhamma-pitaka has provided the basis for most later Buddhist thinking. The Tipitaka is the fundament of Theravada Buddhism.

Study of the scriptures is vital for any Buddhist's understanding of his faith. Laymen, as well as monks, are encouraged to read them, preferably under the aegis of a teacher, who may well know the texts by heart as well as any commentaries. Translations are encouraged, as are public readings. The hearing and absorbing of the scriptures is highly beneficial:

> If anyone ... Accepts, receives and keeps ... this scripture, that person shall never again want for clothing, bedding, food or drink, or for the things to support life ... that person has seen Sakayamuni Buddha.
>
> From the Lotus Sutra

There is an enormous wealth of Buddhist scriptures, most of which are relevant to the respective and differing schools of thought in Buddhism.

THE MAJOR BUDDHIST SCHOOLS

Buddhism gathered followers steadily in the centuries that followed the Buddha's teachings, but until the third century BCE Buddhism scarcely stepped outside northern India. Asoka, an Emperor of the Mauryan dynasty and ruler of much of southern Asia, used Buddhist ideals as his guide for ruling. His son took the doctrine to Ceylon where the first Buddhist scriptures – the Pali Canon – were written down. From Ceylon the faith eventually spread to the other countries in south-east Asia which still follow Theravada Buddhism, one of the two great schools of Buddhism, the other being Mahayana Buddhism.

Theravada Buddhism

Theravada Buddhism, which is the most severe and strict of the two main schools in its application of Buddhist doctrine, deviates little from the original teachings of the Buddha and the Tipitaka. Known as the Doctrine of the Elders, its spread to south-east Asia – where it is dominant in Sri Lanka, Thailand, Burma, Laos and Kampuchea – has also earned it the title of Southern Buddhism.

The emphasis is that the struggle towards nirvana is to be achieved alone and that the ultimate is arhatship. After the death of the body of an enlightened person there is nothing more. There are no rituals nor images (Gotama regarded ritual as useless and even statues of the Buddha are frowned on) – no divine help. It is regarded as useless to pray to the Buddha. How can someone who has achieved the ultimate, has left the world completely, help? For these reasons, this branch of Buddhism does not directly appeal to the masses, but where it exists, it lives happily with the local gods, thus making it acceptable to the ordinary person. But the main thrust of Theravada Buddhism is that salvation, the attainment of arhatship, is for the select few – this is why many followers spend some considerable time in a monastery during their life. The ideal of the Bodhisattva (see Mahayana Buddhism) is rejected utterly. The Theravadin view of nirvana, as written in the Tipitaka, is composed of negatives:

> Nirvana is where there is no earth, water, fire or air. It is not infinite space, nor infinite consciousness. It is not nothing at all, yet it is not the edge of knowing and not-knowing. It is not this world nor the other world, nor is there sun nor moon. It is neither coming nor going nor standing still. It is not the dimness at the end nor the beginning. It has no foundation, no continuation and no stopping. It is the end of suffering.

It is hard to comprehend, but that, after all, is the point. To all those who follow Theravada Buddhism it is, essentially, the only school of thought – because it is directly devolved from the teachings of the great Buddha, Gotama.

Mahayana Buddhism

The second great tradition of Buddhism did not come about with a sudden schism, it was more a gradual levering away. The first signs of a split came, however, at Vesali, during the second Buddhist council (the first was a few months after the liberation of the Buddha) at which the Buddha's teachings were collated in the fourth century BCE. There were elements who wanted to expand out of the strictness of the Theravada and who formed the Mahasanghikas, 'Members of the Great Community', which eventually became the Mahayana school. More liberal than Theravada, Mahayana Buddhism has demonstrated over the centuries a capacity for absorption and transmutation that is not only staggering but has helped it survive in those parts of the world where it still exists: China, Japan, Korea and parts of Asia, and is occasionally known as Eastern Buddhism. By the first century CE it not only covered Nepal, Pakistan and Afghanistan but had penetrated into China. Two centuries later it was the official religion of Korea, and by the sixth century it had arrived in Japan.

As the two schools diverged, the differences became more apparent. The Mahayanists called their school the 'Great Vehicle', following their belief that salvation was open to all mankind. They disparaged the Theravada school by calling it the Hinayana ('Little Vehicle') school, because only the few achieve liberation. Naturally it is thought of – by both sides – as an insult.

Mantrayana Buddhism

In addition to Theravada and Mahayana Buddhism there is a third important school variously known as Mantrayana, Vajrayana (usually translated as the 'Diamond Vehicle') because its essence has the brilliance, the fire and the indestructibility of a diamond), Tantric, Tibetan or Northern Buddhism. Mantrayana Buddhism arrived in Tibet in the seventh century, but was met with resistance by the indigenous shamanistic, ritualistic religion – Bon. The great monk, Padmasambhava, wove a synthesis in the eighth century and it became the official religion of Tibet in the fourteenth century under the reformer Tsong kha pa. His two favourite pupils were the forerunners of the Dalai Lama (the worldly head of Tibetan Buddhism) and the Panchen Lama (the spiritual head).

The development of this school of thought shows Buddhism's extreme adaptability to an extraordinary degree. It originated in great secrecy in India, where it developed from the flowering of sacred tantric literature, some time during the fourth and fifth centuries CE. Basically, it shares the doctrine of Mahayana, but has developed complicated rituals and has overlaid much of the essence of Buddhism with mysticism, occultism and magic.

It uses various specific methods to concentrate the mind in order to attain buddhahood in this life rather than over several. These involve the use of mantras, mudras and mandalas.

Mantras are magic phrases, which, repeated over and over, bring one to a heightened state of consciousness. The potent magic of these mantras may be imagined to spread to the farthest ends of the universe. Writing the mantra on a piece of paper and using a prayer-wheel to give wing to the magic is often practised.

Mudras are ritual gestures which symbolize the desire to be completely at one with the divine. In some places, particularly in Tibet, certain mudras are closely allied with the erotic practices which originated in worship of the Indian goddess Shakti, the eternal feminine – union with whom brings realization of ultimate unity.

Mandalas are circular or many-sided pictures, which represent certain aspects of the cosmic and the spiritual. Meditation on these is designed to bring one to the centre, where one may experience the essence of the divine.

It is a school for initiates only, and may not be followed without adherence to a guru. But the statues, depictions, rituals and ceremonies are highly popular with those who are not initiates. This has contributed to its continuing popularity among the general public.

BUDDHIST FESTIVALS

It could be considered axiomatic that because Buddhists are not really concerned with this world, so the exactness of dates and chronology is of little importance to them. There is no cohesion of dating in Buddhist countries. The Theravadin countries make use of BE, the Buddhist era, dated from the death of Gotama. Chinese and Tibetan Buddhists use a 60-year cycle, in which a combination of the five elements and twelve animals revolve in turn. All Buddhist calendars are a combination of solar and lunar influences, so the working out of the dates of festivals is an expert business. Most Buddhists rely on almanacs for this information. Buddhists also enjoy various secular festivals that are celebrated around the world, provided that they do not directly contradict Buddhist principles.

Uposatha days: almost equivalent to the Christian Sunday. Originally they were held on the new and full moons and were a time for the monks to recite the patimokkha, ethical precepts. Now they are generally used by the laity to spend a day in deeper religious observance.

Rains retreat: in the Theravadin countries this is still strictly observed for three months of the year, roughly July to October. Its history resides in the almost complete impossibility of travel during the monsoon period of northern India and so monks had to stay in one place. For this reason the Mahayana countries do not celebrate it. The end of the retreat, the Kathina ceremony, is celebrated with the laity offering a new robe to one monk, chosen by the abbot. In China, the Rains Retreat became the Summer Retreat and takes place from June to August.

New Year: all Buddhists celebrate New Year, but not necessarily as a religious festival or centred on the monastery or temple. Both the timings and celebrations are different, of course: in Sri Lanka it is the 13 April, the people go home, give presents, have parties; in Thailand it is 13–16 April, in Burma 16 and 17 April, and both countries celebrate with water-throwing ceremonies. In Tibet the first fifteen days of the year commemorate the early life of the Buddha. It is also used as a time for administrative tasks and examinations for the monks. On the final night there are displays, sculpted in butter, of scenes from the life of the Buddha and puppet shows.

All Buddhist countries celebrate the Buddha's Birth, Enlightenment and Death, mostly in May and June, and some all on the same day, while in Sri Lanka, Burma and Tibet the Buddha's First Sermon is celebrated in July.

For the most part, Buddhist festivals, when they are truly Buddhist, centre around the Sangha and take place in temples or monasteries. There are many more minor festivals which take place throughout the spread of Buddhist countries, and are often local in intent.

BUDDHISM TODAY

Somewhere soon after the turn of the thirteenth century CE, Buddhism had all but disappeared from India, overrun by the influx of Islam and a corresponding eruption of Hindu nationalist thought. From the fifteenth century the Theravadin Sangha was astonishingly successful in the countries in south-east Asia where it is still practised, virtually unchanged over the years, with just enough adaptation to endear itself to the local populations. Mayahana Buddhism continues to be well represented in the North. The biggest blow to Buddhism in Tibet came with the annexation of the country by China in 1951 and the exile of the current Dalai Lama. Many monasteries and much culture has been destroyed and the population of the Sangha decimated.

Buddhism – in all its forms – has made a very deep impression in the West since it first arrived towards the end of the nineteenth century. It is admired for its tolerance, its sense of justice, its high ethics and its reliance on self-redemption. Its adaptability, which allowed it such widespread acceptance in the East, particularly in China and Japan, is further proof that Buddhism can truly be considered a worldwide religion.

JAINISM

There is a purity and a lack of compromise about the Jain faith, rooted as it is in an austere asceticism. Jain comes from the Hindu Jina, meaning Conqueror, or Victor; victory over the squalor of life. This is the ultimate aim of all Jains.

Jainism has as long a history as Buddhism and was born into the same part of the world, the Ganges basin in North India, at about the same time. Jainism is rooted, to a certain extent, in this era. In the sixth century BCE the predominant thought was that all sentient things have a soul, which the Jains call jiva, and all jiva are surrounded, in varying degrees, by matter, ajiva. The less enlightened the soul, the heavier the matter. For instance, each rock by the side of the road contains a soul, imprisoned in the densest of matter and unable to cry out if kicked. Through intense discipline and learning and adherence to the truths of Jainism the soul may, by degrees, be liberated from its matter and be freed into the realm of enlightenment. And because the Jains believe that everything has a soul there is an unaccountable number of souls in the universe, most of whom are destined to revolve eternally in the cycle of rebirth, samsara. Only a few of these souls are destined to become human beings and so it is incumbent on these human beings to make the best of themselves, and achieve liberation. It is because the soul is imprisoned in all forms of matter that the injunction of ahimsa – that of actively not harming – is one of the foremost doctrines of Jainism. And although ahimsa is one of the precepts of Hinduism, the Jains take it to a defining extent which has had an influence on the everyday life of the Jain.

The Jain view of the universe, and the relationships of everyone within it, are faintly archaic, but none the less real. They hold that we are gripped by endless, enormous cycles, each lasting 600 million years, of growth and decline. Currently we are in the fifth of six stages of a decline. Although these cycles are immutable, within that each person has the freedom of choice to act his life out according to his own wishes. This is the doctrine of anekantvada (many-sidedness) which posits that viewpoints depend on where you are standing. It is the foundation of the justly famous Jain tolerance. The notion that truth is intensely personal is very Jain, and it is only by recognizing this that you can begin to see the other facets of a case other than your own. This belief frees the Jain religion from any taint of fatalism.

VARDHAMANA MAHAVIRA AND THE HISTORY OF JAINISM

Vardhamana Mahavira (Mahavira is an honorary title meaning great hero) is considered the founder of modern Jainism. He is the last of the 24 great Tirthankaras or fordmakers (those who guide their followers through the pitfalls of life, death and transmigration) of Jainism. Although it is with him that Jain history really begins, his teachings are the development of those 23 Tirthankaras that came before him.

Mahavira came from the Kshatriya (warrior) class, but at about 30 years of age he took up the life of a wandering mendicant, renouncing all family ties and all possessions. He roamed for twelve years, preaching, teaching and discussing. Free from all attachments and encumbrances, he lived a life of utter austerity, according to the ascetic precepts of the followers of the twenty-third Tirthankara, Parsva, who had lived some two hundred and fifty years before. At the end of this time he achieved full liberation and enlightenment. He had beaten the forces of the earthly bonds which bound him to the endless cycles of rebirth and was acclaimed as the twenty-fourth Tirthankara. For the remaining 30-odd years of his life he preached his beliefs and organized his followers. He died of voluntary starvation, a rite known as sallekhana, at Pava, close to his birthplace of Patna.

The earliest followers and contemporaries of Vardhamana Mahavira came, mostly, from his own class. He organized them into highly effective groupings, both lay and monastic. Immediately after his death his disciples spread his teaching from the north-eastern cradle of India, through the north-west and the east. Two or three centuries after Mahavira's death Jainism began to radiate into the central and southern areas of India as well.

The development of the faith was helped by a ruling dynasty which upheld a monastic ideal of auterity, and encouraged the ordinary person of any level of faith – not just the monks – also to uphold that ideal. Jainism in this respect had an advantage over Buddhism in that the lay followers were already the backbone of the faith, and therefore its existence was not dependent on the monastries. The success of the laity meant both that the faith flourished (in spite of the eventual rise of devotional Hinduism and the influx of Islam), and that Jainism has remained peculiarly Indian, with very little proselytizing abroad.

It was during the spread into the centre and the south of India that the major schism in Jainism occurred. The split was about whether Jain monks should be naked or clothed. Undoubtedly Mahavira was unclothed and the Digembaras, meaning 'sky-clad', remain the naked ascetics of Jainism. However, in Gujarat and Rajasthan where the majority of the Shvetambaras ('white clad') now reside, they wear robes.

The story is that at the end of the third century BCE there was a great famine in the north, which led to many of the Jains leaving for the richer lands of the south. When some of them, led by Bhadrabahu (d.357 BCE), returned after about 12 years they found that those left behind were wearing robes. This was considered to be lax discipline – hence the division.

Today, however, many Digambaras do wear robes in public, giving credence to the Shvetambara notion (even in the third century BCE) that because of the degeneration of the world, nude asceticism is not a viable mode of living. When ordained, the Shvetambara monk is given three pieces of cloth, a whisk of wool and a begging bowl. The only possession allowed to a Digambara is a whisk of peacock feathers with which to sweep the path in front of him; thus he removes, gently, any unsuspecting insect in his path.

Most other disagreements centre on the authority of the scriptures, except for one major difference: the Digambaras only allow monks, believing that men may achieve enlightenment, but women must wait for a life in which they are born male. The Shvetambaras do ordain nuns as well as monks. They suppose no difference between the sexes in the ability to reach the goal of liberation from samsara.

Jainism has fluctuated in number of adherents and in area throughout its history, but its stability has been remarkable, in spite of the original split.

JAIN BELIEFS

In common with other Eastern and Indian religions the doctrine of karma is also central. The notion of karma is that every action has a reaction, which in turn induces further action – all of which accumulates and is one of the major reasons why man is prevented from leaving samsara, the eternal cycle of birth and rebirth. Karma ties you to the earth, to the world. And this is particularly the view of the Jains: that karma is literally the accumulation of matter, the more bad karma, the denser your body. Good karma, on the other hand, is dissipated immediately. It may have the effect of rarefying the bad, but the bad karma is best annihilated by conscious deprivation and asceticism.

In other words, the basic understanding of the Jain is that life is all suffering and sadness, and the urgent desire is to leave this world – a literal leaving of the world in all possible material ways. But moksha, liberation, may only be obtained the harshest discipline. This is the only way to free oneself from the karma that binds one to samsara.

There is only one method of release from the dense matter – although it may seem like many, over several lives – and that is to conform to Mahavira's principles of how to live on the earth.

It is the ultimate aim of the Jain to rise above life on earth and, through one's own endeavours, return to the source of all life. But the source of all life is not a god, or indeed gods; it is within one's own true nature. Jainism is essentially atheistic – in its true sense. There are gods, but they are subject to karma and the cycle of samsara as is everyone else. The revered of the Jains are the Tirthankaras, who have, through their own trials attained the longed for release. That they have achieved it means that others might. But the way is long, stony and full of suffering.

The way to salvation starts by following the course of Mahavira's Three Jewels: Right Knowledge, Right Faith and Right Conduct. These are the basic blocks of Jain doctrine. They are inseparable. The difference in application between the lay person and the monk is a question of degree.

All Jains are enjoined in five vows: to abide by ahimsa (the doctrine of doing no harm); to be truthful; not to steal; to abstain as far as possible from sex; and not to desire worldly goods. These five lesser vows for the layman are paralleled by the five great vows for the monk – the same but more stringent because the monk has already given up his possessions, including home and family. Ahimsa, of course, is paramount. He must not harm anything, even accidentally. His speech and thought must ever be truthful, pleasant, devoid of all negativity. He must not ask for nor take anything which is not freely given. He must be chaste. He must renounce and become indifferent to all feeling, thoughts and attachments to the outside and material world. He has an additional injunction not to eat after dark. In all, he must approach his vows with the deepest thought and humility.

The ascetic is a permanent wanderer, without attachments except possibly for an allegiance to one particular community during caturmasa, the rainy season. And although Mahavira was a solitary (ancient texts testify to his way of life) it has proved impractical. The ascetic now wanders as one of many. If by chance he is solitary, then he is assumed to be a deviant, or that it is a temporary phase or perhaps a punishment.

The reasons for renunciation are varied. It might come from an innate desire to renounce the world, to free oneself from poverty or other binding emotions or the appeal of an ascetic life or ritual; it might be a dream or a promise or a memory of previous lives; it might be enlightenment, inspiration or example by a god or a teacher; it might be the time of life. For a nun it may be to escape marriage or widowhood. It is open to all classes, except (inescapable in India) the lowest.

The whole point of the ascetic life is to prevent the influx of new karma and to eradicate what is already there by restraint and forbearance. There are two motivations – care in action and the establishment of positive qualities. Being this austere is regarded as something special, difficult, conferring a particular dignity or nobility. The Tirthankaras regarded austerity as the cure to the 'illness of transmigration'. Buddhists regard asceticism as the result of bad karma; the Jains maintain that one can only become an ascetic having rid oneself of most karma, because the ascetic is single-minded in concentration and goal. Meditation, fasting and devotion were transforming powers in the Jain ethic.

There are six obligatory actions in the ritual of the ascetic: equanimity, repentance, abandonment, laying down the body, prayer and praise and the act of homage. These, always necessary in the life of the ascetic, also developed into a cogent liturgy and ritual for the laity, which follows the precepts of the ascetic, as far as it can. That both monk and layman followed these rituals proved the validity of the path.

The interaction between the ascetic and the laity – always there, if a necessary compromise as far as the ascetic was concerned – is constant and has developed over the years into something more than minimal. Today the layman often follows the ascetic on his travels, providing for him in various ways, and easing his path. The most obvious interaction is in alms-giving. Giving – dana – is worthy in any faith but in the Jain doctrine it is prestigious. The monk is revered – sometimes as if he himself were an image of Tirthankara. In return the monk, by the very existence of his mode of life, embodies the perfection of Jain tenets. Each side should be as pure as can be.

For both the ascetic and the layman there is a possible way of eliminating much karma, particularly when close to the end of a life. This is by the rite of sallekhana, the fasting to death. It is the religious death, and the method, as well as the state of the person at the moment of passing, determines the next birth. Sallekhana is regarded as the purest possible way of dying, being both solitudinous and difficult. Because of the prevailing climate it is not practised today; the last monk died in this way in 1955. But as an ideal it is still upheld.

The lay estate was accepted by the Jains as a vocation in its own right. The laity was necessary as the support for the growing Jain ascetic community. Now, while the ascetic continues to look for release, the layman looks for a good life and a better birth. He still follows the five vows of the ascetic, but balances them against the exigencies of modern life.

It is in the doctrine of ahimsa, however, that the most obvious restrictions on the life of a Jain layman are seen. He must be vegetarian, he may follow no profession that will actively harm any living being, so farming is not possible, neither are trades such as carpentry, cobbling or metalworking.

The safest profession for a Jain is trade. Interestingly, the proportion of wealthy Jains is higher than might be expected given their very small percentage of the total Indian population. This is due to various factors: the responsibility and austerity of the religion; the network of religion and caste; a reputation for probity. The external show of piety and restraint, modesty and reticence, delivers the inner piety. This, as much as anything else, is the Jain layman, even today.

THE JAIN SCRIPTURES

'The Worthy One enunciates the meaning, then the disciples form the sacred text, and then the sacred text proceeds for the good of the doctrine.'
Attributed to Bhadrabahu

This is a rough approximation of the Sanskrit word, *agama*, which designates an 'arrived' body of doctrine, transmitted orally by undisputed teachers. For many Jains the fact of having scriptures is more important than having read them – it underlines the historic tradition of their faith. This is in spite of the fact that very few of the scriptures are original, having been written during various recensions – as late as 800 years after Mahavira's death. Early Jain historians, disappointed that the texts were later than they would have liked them to be, concocted the occasional story of 'discovery' to prove antiquity.

At first the scriptures and teachings were handed down through the oral tradition (which Bhadrabahu was the last to know perfectly), but it was not until the fifth century CE that the canon was formalized according to the Shvetambara tradition. Collectively this canon is known as the Siddhanta and contains the writings, angas, supposed to have come directly from Mahavira. However, the Digambaras rejected this canon as inauthentic in language and form, although some of it is a direct transliteration from the oral flowery prose of early CE Sanskrit poesy. The Digambaras do, however, hold to the precepts contained in the scriptures – for them it is the metaphysical application of the writings, rather than the words themselves, which are important. It is believed that there are earlier lost scriptures, common to both sects.

The Shvetambara canon consists of 45 texts, classified into five groups. The first group is the anga, the 12-limbed canon, reduced to 11 (the Drishtivada, the Disputation about Views, is lost), in the first recension in 368 BCE. For the classical Jain the scripture resembles the 12 limbs, anga, of man – feet, calves, thighs, forearms, arms, neck and head. The anga is an exposition of the range of Jain beliefs, doctrine, practice, mythology, cosmology, plus stories of those who transcended samsara and those who became Gods. The second group is the upanga, the twelve subsidiary limbs, which expound further on these subjects, and include discussions between kings and monks. The third is the Seven (of which the sixth is lost) Chedasutras which outline the ascetic life of a monk and the monastic law; the fourth, Four Mula Sutras (the basic scriptures) must be read by all aspiring monks; the fifth is the mixed sutras, the prakirnaka, containing (among other subjects) monastic ritual, praise of the fordmakers, the practice of sallekhana (religious suicide). To these 43 texts two were added in the fifth century CE, the Nandi and Anuyogadvarani. These are concerned with exposition, interpretation and theory.

The Digambaras have their own canon which they consider to be the only authentic one, because they believe all scriptures are lost except for two : the Scripture in Six Parts (Shatkhandagama) and the Treatise on the Passions (Kashayaprabhrta). In essence these differ little from the Shvetambara canon, either in content or in form and appear to be contemporary with the Shvetambara writings. Both canons divided the writings into kalika (texts which may be studied only at certain times) and utkalika (those texts which may be read at any time).

There is one further book that is considered seminal by the Jain and that is the Kalpa Sutra, written by Bhadrabahu in the fourth century BCE. It contains, in brief, the lives of the 23 Tirthankaras, a list of early sixth century BCE monks and their code of conduct, but, most importantly, it contains a detailed biography of Mahavira.

Very few Jains have read the scriptures – the Ardhamagadhi language is not easy, and it was considered unwise for the ordinary Jain to be exposed to such works without the requisite amount of learning; in fact many erudite Jains insisted that the oldest scriptures could not be understood by *anyone* who lived in the corrupt world. These scriptures could therefore only be venerated as religious objects. And in spite of the translation of the scriptures, there is still some conflict today between those who would preserve scriptures (particularly those written on palm leaves) as sacred objects, and those who would view the same scriptures as a clue to history.

There is still a lot of work to be done in the field of exposition and dissemination of all the Jains texts. That it has not been done in any truly systematic fashion is surprising, considering that the Jains have the oldest libraries in India. The earliest date from the eleventh century CE and the first recorded catalogue dates from 1383. But access has been limited, partly through fear of loss and partly due to the belief that the writings were beyond the average person. Proof used to be needed of Jain lineage – preferably to a major teacher – before access was granted. These Jain libraries contain a wealth of literature, Indian as well as Jain, just waiting to be discovered.

JAIN RITUAL AND WORSHIP

Jains congregate frequently in the numerous and beautiful Jain temples. Although it is to revere the images of the Tirthankaras, it is not worship as outsiders might see it. The object of revering the images is not to ask for mundane help or intercession (for this, Jains turn to the Hindu gods), it is a question of gaining inspiration from devotion by those who have already attained moksha. The devotions to these images serve as a focus through which Jains may effect internal change. The statue essentially represents all fordmakers and their qualities, and therefore, by extension, the god to be found within all. The real worship for the Jain lies in the austerity of fasting, both in participation and glorification. But all Jains make puja, homage, either in the temples, or in a home shrine, to their images. It is not a communal exercise, rather it is intensely personal and undertaken without acknowledgement of any other worshipping Jains present.

It is the spirit in which the image is approached which is the most important element in temple or shrine obeisance. Gifts may be given, except by the poor or the ascetic, but it is the concentration of the mind on the qualities that the particular image embodies that is more important. There are, however, certain devotions that are carried out by the layman or the temple functionaries. On entering the temple or the shrine the word nihishi, meaning abandonment, is whispered. This embodies the move from one world to another and is said again when passing from the outer temple to the inner sanctum. After walking round the image three times, the follower washes the statue with water (this signifies the purity of a soul freed from karma), anoints it with camphor and sandalwood (the quieting of the mind) and makes an offering of a garland of flowers (the attainment of the 'fragrance' of the Three Jewels).

Then he withdraws to the main hall to carry out the last five elements of the puja. (This last may be practised as a small puja on its own, without the earlier purification of the image). Incense is swung (the burning of karmic matter), lamps are waved (attainment of enlightenment) and the puja is completed by the laying out, in a ritual fashion, of the offerings of fruit, sweets and rice (the intention to live one's life in the proper Jain manner).

The rice is laid out in designs that signify the tenets of the Jain faith. First: the sign of the Indian swastika, the four corners representing the four states of existence – human, god, animal, and hellbeing. Then, above that, horizontally, three dots for the Three Jewels, and above that a crescent with a single dot – this signifies the Curving Place at the top of the world where the liberated souls reside.

After this the spare food is eaten. In Hinduism, the food is eaten in order to absorb some of the qualities of the deity who is assumed to have 'eaten' it first. The Jains eat it precisely because it has been *not* eaten but *rejected* by the fordmakers, and therefore its ingestion confers an asceticism. The steps of the puja exemplify the lay Jain's desire to continue his spiritual development and his deep commitment to the faith's ideal of renunciation.

In spite of Jainism being profoundly atheistic, its followers have built some of the most remarkable temples all over India. Many of them are places of pilgrimage – not linked to the worship of relics but rather with the attaining of enlightenment. And although many of them are by water and were built in honour of the fordmakers, the Jains do not hold, unlike the Hindus, that water has deep and sacred properties of purity. The act of travelling and pilgrimage confers merit but is not a requirement of the Jain faith. Its main principle is that it allows the Jain to become an ascetic for a time. It is also popular because it mixes fun with faith and is an opportune time for Jains to be together communally.

Festivals the world over are designed to bring people together with a common purpose. Unlike the wild exuberance of Hindu festivals, however, the Jains prize restraint even in their celebrations. There are immunerable events in the Jain calendar, most of which are relatively small and regional All last for only a day (except Paryushana) and all have to do with celebrating important people and events in the history of the religion, but there is little synchronicity between the dating of these events by the two main sects of Jainism. Except for one:

that is the Mahavira Jayanti which takes place in April. This festival celebrates both Mahavira's descent into his mother's womb and his birth. All the other festivals, such as the Immortal Third and the Scripture Fifth (which honour the first alms-giving and the first committing of the scriptures in writing respectively) are celebrated on different dates by Shvetambara and Digambara.

Even the most important festival, that of the end of the year, Paryushana, is celebrated on different days for differing lengths of time. It falls during July and August in the rainy season, when the weather obliges the monks and nuns to remain in one place. It provides some of the best opportunities for a deep and close interaction between the ascetic and lay communities, reinforcing their mutual dependence and encouraging each to grow in devotion and understanding. The layman fasts and attends special services and many adopt the practices of the monks, spending twenty-four hours in a monastery, fasting and meditating. The last day of the festival is always a fast and on the same evening all gather in the local temple and ask for any transgressions to be forgiven. No Jain wishes to go into the New Year with any hint of grudge or quarrel attached to him or her.

Jains join Hindus in celebrating Diwali, the festival of lights. However, they have adapted it as the anniversary of Mahavira's death and liberation – the occasion of Mahavira's seeing of the light.

JAINISM TODAY

There have been throughout the history of the Jain religion many intellectual exponents of the faith, all of whom have sought to underline, on a textual basis, everything that a Jain has done or believed. Some of the more notable ones are Bhadrabahu who, in the third century BCE wrote the Kalpa Sutra; the eighth-century Haribhadrasuri who wrote 1,444 treatises on the scriptures; Hemchandracharya (1088–1172 CE) who wrote dozens of scholarly books on history, poetry, yoga, mythology, philosophy and who developed the grammar of the Prakrit language from which Gujarati is derived; Hirvijaysuri, who, in the sixteenth century, was close to the Muslim Emperor Akbar and gained concessions for the Jain faith by his wisdom and preaching; the seventeenth-century philosopher Yashovijayji who wrote on logic and ritual and who is still read today, and Shrimad Rajchandra (1867–1901) who, although not a monk, renounced everything and devoted himself to the examination of texts – much of his work is still regarded as seminal by all Jains. The arguments of these scholars have kept the intellectual rigour of the faith alive, while the laity has always maintained the fact of the faith.

The Jains are relatively few in number in total, perhaps two million worldwide. It has never been a proselytizing religion, serving to attract by example. It is a curious fact that the Jains wield remarkable influence for such a small group, and, for the most part, are both wealthy and influential. Mahatma Gandhi drew from the Jains in his philosophy, particularly the Jain doctrine of ahimsa. They are great promoters of public welfare, donating and building schools and hospitals, and have adapted well to the modern technological age. One problem does face the Jains, however: that of reconciling the immediacy of living in the world today with the deep asceticism that is the root of Jainism. But it is likely, given that the doctrinal tenets of the faith are so deeply imbued in the Jain psyche, that they will find the way. It seems improbable that the ultimate and admirable goal of the Jains – to expand beyond the here and now and fasten on the need to return to the state of original being – will be lost to the future.

SIKHISM

There is only one God, whose name is truth, who is the all-pervading Creator, without fear, without hate, without time, without form. He is beyond birth and death, he is self-enlightened. He is known by the grace of the Guru.

Adi Granth 1, the Mul Mantra

This is the first verse in the scriptures, the Adi Granth, and the foundation of the Sikh religion.

Sikhism is one of the youngest of the world religions, being a fraction less than 500 years old. It is an immensely practical religion – perhaps more than any other it is for living in this world. It is not about enlightenment as is understood in those religions whose only joy is in leaving the world, it is about being the best possible in this world. To do this a belief in God and the divine intent of God's will are uttermost.

The concept of the Guru is at the centre of the Sikh faith. And the Guru of all Gurus – Satguru – is God, the one God with thousands of names, who, although unknowable and incomprehensible, spoke to the Sikh community first through the ten great Gurus, then through the Adi Granth and finally through the whole of the Sikh community, panth, itself. So, in a sense, the community, the direct human experience, embodies God.

SIKH BELIEFS

For the Sikh it is axiomatic that God is unknowable, without form, nirankar, and without qualities, nirguna, and not made manifest in any way, has not been an avatar, has not shown himself in human form. He is the creator of everything known and unknown and is immanent and transcendent – Sikhs do not consider a God who is separate from his creations. He is an intensely personal God, but this is not personal in the sense of exclusive, just that he is available to anyone who is willing to let him in.

There is no rigid doctrinal system to force a believer into a strict moral code. The development of Sikh doctrines owes less to academic exercise than to the expression of direct human experiences of God, both in daily life and in spiritual applications.

To know God in the Sikh faith is to be devotional, to meditate on the name of God, to gather together in groups and praise him through song and prayer, to ask that he be present in his unknowable form in the heart. In prayer, a Sikh does not meditate on any image, but on the abstract purity experienced by devotion. When the Adi Granth, the scriptures, talks of how 'beauteous are the Lord's eyes, sparkling his teeth, graceful is thy gait, O Lord, sweet thy speech' (Adi Granth, 567/10) it is not intended as a figurative representation of God. It is only man's way of trying to understand and express the numinousness of God.

There is no requirement for asceticism, nor for leaving the family and community. God may be found in everyday life, He is not sought apart and out of the way. The striving for nirvana, for release from the earth-bound, is by finding God in your heart by the way you live your life. You may live while you love God. Denial is not part of the contract, except that it is as well to leave behind excessive longing for material goods – overdue attachment to the accumulation of material goods tends to blunt the capacity for recognizing God. Moderation is the key.

God is merciful and God will accept anyone who turns to him in the right way. There are two concepts, munmakh and gurmukh – person-centred and God-centred. The idea is to let God, not self, become the centre. By coming together with others of like mind, or with others who have already found God in themselves, the worshipper will be encouraged to discover his own God-self, through the medium of hymns, prayers and general devotions.

In common with all the other Indian religions, Sikhs believe that the soul does not die, nor can it be destroyed, unlike the body which it inhabits. Yet body and soul are complimentary. All beings are endowed with soul, but only mankind has been given the understanding of the world and its environment and the ability to make choices, to distinguish between right and wrong. This is his free will. But inherent in the teachings of the Gurus is the notion of submitting to God's will – life will be easier and suffering less, if you abide by God's rules.

The nature of Sikhism is virtually inextricable from its history. Therefore the progressions of its beliefs, doctrines and rituals are best explained through the historical development of the faith, the lives of the Ten Gurus and through the scriptures, the Adi Granth.

GURU NANAK AND THE HISTORY OF SIKHISM

Sikhism springs from the Punjab, in north-west India, which had been under Muslim domination for some four centuries. There was little climate of integration between the two major religions of Hinduism and Islam; for the most part each led their completely separate lives. The founder of Sikhism, Guru Nanak (1468–1539 CE), was an unlikely propagator of a religion in one sense, in that he was an accountant (employed by the local Muslim governor) and from the Kshatriya class. But he was always a contemplative man, with a religious cast of mind, rather than one of action.

Guru Nanak did not set out to form a new movement, nor did he intend, at first, that his life should follow its eventual path. It was an intense mystical experience that moved him toward his understanding of the nature of the Divine. He vanished for three days (causing a search and even a dragging of the river where he had been bathing), after which he returned to his family and pronounced that 'There is no Muslim or Hindu – so which path shall I follow? God is neither Muslim nor Hindu and so I shall follow God's path.'

God, he felt, was beyond any religious structures. He was to be found within the heart of each and every person rather than by strict adherence to any religious doctrine. Guru

Nanak's teachings have been construed by some as a deliberate attempt to blend the two prevailing religions, to meld the Indian concept of karma into the monotheism of Islam. But as he was critical of certain pronouncements made in the name of these and other religions, it is far more likely that he was never consciously attempting anything – rather that his mystical experience pointed to a simpler, more attainable understanding of God.

Guru Nanak spent several years as a wandering preacher, drawing congregations wherever he went. He eventually settled at Kartarpur where he founded a community based on a simple religious life of devotion and praise of God, while living a normal life and going about normal business: the concept of a constant mindfulness of God in everyday life. Certain procedures were established, such as ritual purification before morning prayer and the eating of a communal meal after evening worship.

One of Guru Nanak's early visitors at Kartarpur was Bhai Lehna, an adherent of the Hindu god Durga. Lehna (b. 1504, Guru 1539–52) was so overwhelmed by the spiritual essence of the place that he bound himself immediately to the Sikh faith. His devotion, commitment and purity were such that Guru Nanak gave him the name of Angad (limb). He nominated Angad as his successor. This established the concept of guruship with each successive Guru nominating the next. For the Sikh each Guru is part of the same soul, indistinguishable from one another.

Guru Angad built on the precepts of his predecessor, giving shape to the vision of Guru Nanak. He is credited with being the founder of the Gurmukhi (from the mouth of the Guru) script, in which all the Sikh hymns and scriptures are written. This, followed by the opening of Sikh schools, was probably done with the intention of separating the Sikhs from the influence of the Hindu brahmins. There was also, at the time, a drive in certain quarters towards asceticism, which was against all that Guru Nanak had taught. Guru Angad not only emphasized the supreme importance of family life but also the necessity of physical fitness, particularly wrestling and sports. Although no follower was actually trained in the art of warfare, its foundations were established for when the call, later, actually came.

Guru Angad died young and his successor Amar Das (b.1479, Guru 1552–74) both deepened and broadened the scope of the Sikh faith as a separate ideal. He instituted the langar, the notion of commensality – the communal meal. This was one of the truest attempts to take the caste out of Sikh society. It is a meal, open to all, regardless of sex or class, and the fact that it has not entirely succeeded in its aim is less due to any failings in Sikhism than it is to do with inherent entrenched divisions in social India.

Guru Amar Das ordained that there should be Sikh gatherings on Hindu festival days. He appointed women – as well as men – as missionaries. He replaced the Sanskrit verses in the birth and death rituals with Sikh hymns. His most famous hymn, the Anand Sahib, is now included in the daily worship of the Sikhs.

> Your name, O Lord, is my sustenance,
> I live only on the true name, which calms all my hungers
> The true name, abiding in my heart,
> Has given me peace and joy, and fulfilled all my desires.
> I am ever a sacrifice to the Guru, whose gifts these are.
> Nanak says, listen O Saints, love the word.
> Your name, O Lord, is my sustenance.
>
> Adi Granth, 917

There was, however, one ritual he promoted which came with him from his Hindu upbringing and that was the idea of ritual cleansing – just as Guru Nanak insisted that the inner self be cleansed with prayer, so Guru Amar Das insisted on outer cleansing before conversing with God. Cleansing before prayers is still a part of the Sikh ritual today.

Amar Das' successor was his son-in-law, Ram Das (b.1534, Guru 1574–81). He is remembered mostly for his wedding hymns (so obviating the need for Hindu brahmins to officiate) and for the foundation of Amritsar in 1577 and the digging of the pool in which Harimandir (the house of God), the eventual Golden Temple, would be built. Amritsar was to become one of the central foci of the Sikh religion. It was the start of the deep identification of the Sikh with the Punjab as homeland.

Ram Das's youngest son, Arjan, (b.1581–1606) was the first Guru to have been born a Sikh. Arjan had a fondness for physical fitness, wrestling and fencing matches, and was the first Guru to combine the mystical and the physical, composing over 2,000 hymns which form the main body of Adi Granth. He completed the building of Harimandir in the pool at Amritsar and placed in it the compilation of sacred writings of the Sikhs. Guru Arjan's completion of this temple consolidated the foundations of his predecessors: Sikhism had its own language, ritual and scriptures and now a central place of worship.

But trouble was brewing in India, and Arjan's ministry was in the centre of it. In 1525 the Muslim Mughal Empire had been established in northern India under Babur. In the beginning, relations between the Sikh panth and the ruling Muslims were tolerable, particularly under the rule of Akbar (1556–1605) who sought to unite a cultural India by allowing indigenous faiths freedom to practise. With Akbar's death the country, including the Sikh community, was embroiled in a war of succession: Akbar's son, Jehangir, against *his* son, Khusrau.

Guru Arjan was killed by Jehangir while in custody. For various reasons – including the closeness and idealism of the Sikh community – he *and the whole panth* were perceived as a threat by Jehangir. It is at this point that the emphasis of the panth turned from the purely pacific and religious to include the militaristic and defensive. From here Guru Angad's insistence on physical prowess in games and sports was to prove far-sighted, for Guru Arjan's successor, his youngest son Hargobind (b.1595, Guru 1606–44), raised his own army to defend the Sikh way of life.

Guru Hargobind outlived Jehangir only to fall foul of Shah Jehan. Although a reasonably tolerant ruler, Shah Jehan objected to Guru Hargobind's encouragement of the Sikhs to train in the art of warfare and imprisoned the Guru for some years in the fort at Gwalior. After his release, Guru Hargobind decided to remove himself from the jurisdiction of the Mughal rulers and left Amritsar for Kiratpur in the foothills of the Himalayas. Here he developed the concept of the two

113

swords, miri and piri – the combination of temporal and spiritual power. So Sikhism became synonymous not only with nam, mindfulness, and familial responsibility, but also with the armed struggle against oppression.

Guru Hargobind's successors, the seventh, eighth and ninth Gurus, were not militant, but his warlike mantle was taken on in no uncertain terms by his grandson, Guru Gobind Rai (b.1666, Guru 1675–1708). He inherited not only the flame of guruship but also the essence of the combative principle. From an early age he was interested in military games – alongside a well-developed sense of injustice. He maintained that the duty of a Sikh was not necessarily to engage in battle against another race or religion, but against oppression and evil in whatever guise and wherever they may be found.

The core of teaching which came from Guru Nanak provided the basis on which all the other Gurus built. Guru Gobind Rai capitalized on this ethical structure by the creation of the Khalsa (which means pure) – a deliberate challenge to the ruling of Aurangzeb (Shah Jehan's son) that only the traditional warrior class might own horses and bear arms.

On 30 March 1699, the day of the spring harvest, the Guru gathered his followers together at Anandpur. He called for five men to make the ultimate sacrifice of their lives in the cause of the faith. At first, no one was willing, but then, Daya Ram, a warrior, entered the tent with the Guru. The waiting crowd heard a thud, then saw the Guru reappear with a bloody sword. Daya Ram was followed by four men, all from different classes. The thud was heard four more times, each one making the crowd more uneasy, but with the last appearance of the Guru and the sword came the five men, alive and unharmed.

The Guru explained that these sacrifices were symbolic. He needed the community to be clear that the faith was worth fighting for, that oppression must be resisted – sometimes to the point of death. The men were dressed in identical clothing, saffron robes with a blue sash and turbans. They were to be the first five members of the new community of the Khalsa and would be known as the Beloved Five – *panj pyare*.

The Guru initiated the five men with *amrit* (blessed water sweetened with sugar), after which many more came forward for initiation and rebirth into the new community of the Khalsa and changed their names. Each man was to take the name of Singh (Lion), each woman the title of Kaur (Princess), and to dispense with their given names which were linked to matters of caste. The Guru himself changed his name to Guru Gobind Singh.

The Khalsa members had to follow cardinal rules of conduct, which included the wearing of the five Ks: Keshas – unshorn beards and uncut hair, a mark of dedication and holiness; Kangha – a comb, essential for cleanliness, one of the Sikh precepts; Kaccha – short trousers, more modest and practical; Kara – a steel bracelet worn on the right wrist, to protect the sword arm and Kirpan – the sword, symbolizing dignity and respect, the willingness to fight in defence of truth or against oppression. In addition to the wearing of the turban by men (and women, if they so wished), Khalsa members vowed to abstain from drugs and intoxicants; to respect women (no rape or adultery); to reject caste and to regard all Khalsa members as brothers and sisters; to follow the teachings of the Guru, and to serve only the Guru, with arms if necessary and in a just cause. As Guru Gobind said: 'When all other means have failed it is right to draw the sword.'

Apart from the creation of the Khalsa, the other great achievement of Guru Gobind Singh was that he did not designate a successor. Instead he nominated the Sikh panth, the Khalsa and, most importantly, the scriptures, the Adi Granth. These last were invested with guruship, were to be known as the Guru Granth Sahib and were to be the arbiter of all the Sikhs. This book was to have holy pride of place.

THE SIKH SCRIPTURES

From the Timeless One came the bidding
By which the panth was established
All Sikhs are commanded:
Acknowledge as Guru the Granth.
Acknowledge the Granth as Guru,

The manifest body of the Gurus.
You whose hearts are pure,
Seek him in the word.

These lines are said daily at the end of Ardas, the Sikh prayers, and embody the position that the Adi Granth (meaning first and original book) holds in the faith. The Sikh scriptures are central to Sikh religious belief and practice, more so, perhaps, than any other religion. Because they also enshrine the concept of the Guru's body made manifest in words, they are more often known as the Guru Granth Sahib, the book of the Guru. It is the ultimate guide of everything that happens in the life of a Sikh. It is the focus of worship in the gurdwara (temple) and at the centre of every ritual and rite of passage in the Sikh calendar. To a great extent it is now the object on which all Sikhs meditate – in spite of Guru Nanak's original injunctions that outward forms of religion were pointless unless the heart were right. Most people, after all, need something on which to concentrate.

It plays a central role in the principal Sikh rites of passage – the naming of babies, initiation, marriage, death. In every case listening to a reading of the Guru Granth Sahib is as if listening to the Gurus themselves, as if maintaining a dialogue with them, and asking for help and encouragement through all the joys and difficulties of life.

Each and every copy of the Guru Granth Sahib is identical in layout, consisting of 1,430 pages, regardless of size, so if you turn to page 345 or 543 you will see the same words written in every edition. The style is poetic; the emphasis is on mystical application as a guide to seeing God. It contains no lives of the Gurus, nor any historical references – except for a mention of Babur, the first Mughal emperor – nor a guide to ethics. It is a collection of devotional hymns (of which there are nearly 5,900) composed by the Gurus and arranged in ragas (verses), most of which are meant to be sung. Sikhs are particularly proud, however, that hymns from poets and mystics of other faiths – such as the Muslims Kabir and Farid and the Hindus Namdev and Jaidev – are included. Underlying this is the Sikh tenet that no one religion has the true monopoly on faith: God's grace is available to all with the right heart.

The book occupies a special place in the gurdwara, or temple. There are certain rites which pertain to its use which stem from its original placement in the Harimandir (Golden Temple) in 1604. The Granth is installed on a raised 'throne' under a canopy. It is given further respect by the waving of a chauri (a fan of yak tail hair which is a symbol of authority), and covered when not in use. Certain members of the congregation (those whose lives are exemplary) are chosen to act as a granthi. The granthi is entrusted with the duty of care for the Guru Granth Sahib and with the readings and other ceremonies in the gurdwara. When it is too worn to be read any more it is cremated and the ashes scattered into a rive – as befits the death of any great Guru.

The Guru Granth Sahib has been translated from the Punjabi into Urdu, Hindi, English and French. But all ceremonies are carried out in the original Punjabi. This ensures that the language, wherever the Granth is consulted in the world, will remain one of the unifying factors of the Sikhs of the Punjab.

After the Guru Granth Sahib, the most important scripture is the Dasam Granth, the Book of the Tenth Master. These are a collection of the hymns of Guru Gobind Singh – which he did not include in the Adi Granth when he was compiling the final edition, which includes the hymns of his father, Teg Badahur. Again, each edition of the Dasam Granth is identical. It also contains the jap – meditation – which forms part of the daily prayers of the Sikh.

SIKH WORSHIP

The Sikh is enjoined both to meditate alone and to worship communally – the latter being an important part of binding the panth together, and is characteristic of the Sikh faith. Guru Nanak emphasized the importance of sangat (congregation): by associating with the good, one becomes good. Communal worship takes place in the gurdwara – and anywhere that has ceremonially installed the Guru Granth Sahib is a gurdwara.

The original buildings (known as dharamsalas, places for the practice of dharma, righteousness) were modest so as not to attract the attention of the Muslim rulers. The first proper temples were built in defiance, culminating in the jewel, the Golden Temple at Amritsar. In India the temples are open from dawn to dusk. Worshippers may enter to listen to a reading, to pray, or to read from the Granth themselves. Anyone may read from the Granth, although occasionally a gurdwara might employ the services of a granthi – a reader who is specially trained.

There are no priests as such. When a gurdwara is established someone has to be appointed to look after it and the person selected is a respected member of the community, going by the title of bhaiji (brother). His most important duty is to be up early and arrange the morning prayer. There are other ceremonial duties which are shared with the rest of the elected management committee.

But wherever in the world a gurdwara may be, the form of the service is almost identical. Whole families attend the gurdwara. Shoes are removed, the head is covered. No tobacco is carried in and anyone who is drunk is asked to leave. The Guru Granth Sahib is approached with offerings (money, flowers or food for the kitchen), and is then revered by bowing or prostrating. The worshipper will move backwards, without turning his back on the scripture, and seat himself on the floor. There is no distinction made of any difference in religious affiliation or social status, but although the sexes worship together, the women sit separately. This is due more to ancient social tradition than to religious edict: they are expected to look after the children and keep them quiet during the service. They are not veiled and are free to move around and chat. All worshippers tend to come and go as they please.

Worship starts with a reading. The Guru Granth Sahib is opened at random and the lesson is taken from the first passage on the left-hand page. This is the thought for the day. The reading continues until the reader considers that enough people are present for the kirtan – the singing of hymns accompanied by music. After kirtan there is katha – an explanation of the hymn chosen by the reader. He also has to keep the congregation informed about social and political issues and other concerns of the community. It matters not what the subject is, the only criterion is that a spiritual atmosphere must prevail: he may start his address with the statement, 'The Khalsa belongs to God, Victory belongs to God.'

At the end of the service the congregation will stand for Ardas — literally, petition. It is the blessing of the service, recalling the sacrifices made in the name of the faith, calling for forgiveness and enlightenment. This is followed by langar — a full vegetarian meal and the final lesson, during which karah prasad (a cooked mixture of flour, sugar and clarified butter) is distributed.

Sikh Festivals

Guru Amar Das commanded the Sikh panth to congregate at Baisakhi and Diwali in order that they might show their allegiance to the Guru rather than to the Hindu brahmins. Guru Gobind Singh added the third, Hola Mohalla, on the Hindu festival of Holi.

Baisakhi is the first of the three festivals in the Sikh calendar and the most important. It commemorates not only the spring and the occasion of the creation of the first Khalsa but also two other historical events when the Sikhs took up arms. Since then Baisakhi is also a time for political as well as spiritual speeches. Baisakhi is also the day when the gurdwara flag, the nisan sahib (the Khalsa emblem on a saffron base), is renewed and the flagpole cleaned.

Sikhs share Diwali (the festival of lights, in October/November), which is an all-India festival, with the Hindus. For the Sikhs, however, it is the time of autumn-cleaning and of bringing the beds back inside before the cool of winter. They also remember that the founding of Amritsar was begun in this month, and the Golden Temple is lit by hundreds of lights.

Hola Mohalla (February/March) was ordained by Guru Gobind Singh so that Sikhs could celebrate the Hindu festival of Holi in their own manner. Anandpur is the principal place of the festivities, which take the form of sports and tournaments, harking back to the days when Hola Mohalla (literally 'attack and place of attack') was an exercise in military manoeuvres.

Apart from these three major festivals, there are the gurpurbs, the birth or death anniversaries of the Gurus. Usually only the major centenaries are celebrated in any big way. Then there is a continuous reading of the Guru Granth Sahib, the end of which coincides with the start of the festival.

SIKHISM TODAY

By the beginning of the nineteenth century there was precious little evidence of true Sikhism in India. For Sikh religious values and culture had become subsumed in the dominant Hindu culture – the gurdwaras were administered by Hindus and marriages performed according to Hindu regulations. Even a Sikh homeland established in the Punjab had lasted for only 50 years. In the latter part of the nineteenth century, however, the proselytizing of Christian and Hindu missionaries in the Punjab provoked the Sikhs into a serious and reinvigorating espousal of their own faith. They formed the Singh Sabha, small groups to counter the threat of the missionaries and to educate Sikhs in the Sikh tradition. They set up schools, invoked the dominance of the Guru Granth Sahib and did everything possible to encourage the continuance of their faith. The successful promotion of a separate Sikh identity resulted in the Anand Marriage Act of 1909 and the Gurdwara Act of 1925.

There is a move toward Sikh secession of the Punjab, to a total identification of the faith with ethnicity. Indeed, Sikh ethnicity has a long history. The second Guru did invent the Gurmurkhi script as the first step in freeing the Sikhs from Hindu bonds. And successive Gurus carried on the tradition of separation. But from an objective viewpoint, secession sits none too easily with Guru Nanak's vision of all being welcome to God, regardless of race or creed.

Meanwhile many Sikhs have emigrated to live in other countries. They have taken with them their customs and beliefs and have often influenced their adopted communities with their concept of spirituality. Some customs have gone – a Sikh may well be a tobacconist these days and not all Sikhs leave their hair uncut or grow beards. Some do not even wear turbans – one of the ultimate symbols of the faith. But with wider dissemination of the ideals of a faith which is immensely practical, as well as spiritual and loving, there are more young people turning toward traditional ideals. Often this happens to children whose parents have espoused the Western way of life more than their contemporaries. Guru Nanak would approve – the perfect counter to the excessive materialism of the West and the worst of its influences.

3 • THE DIVERSITY OF THE FAR EAST

RELIGIONS IN CHINA

There are three main religions in China: two are indigenous, Confucianism and Taoism, the third, Buddhism, is imported. Over four millennia these strands have intermingled (not always happily, of course) to provide a syncretism that is almost paralleled by the example of Japan. But the religions of China are unique in that, until the coming of Buddhism, they have flowered without any outside interference of rite or ideology. They are truly Chinese and born from the Chinese character.

The earliest recorded religion is the magical, shamanistic, divinatory religion of the great Shang dynasty (c.1766–1122 BCE), the first dynasty about which anything much is known. It was a religion in which belief in spirits and magical divination predominated. Answers to kingly questions were divined by a shaman from the shoulder blades of an ox or the shell of a tortoise. The will of the spirits informed everything the Shang wished to do.

The Chou dynasty (c.1122–325 BCE) developed the cult of the spirit of the bones into a more formalized ancestor worship. The reverence for the ancestor was partly the forerunner of the Confucian notion of filial piety and duty which was the basis for his view of the need for ethical and gentlemanly conduct in everyday life.

At the same time, there was a pervasive belief during both these dynasties in the forces and balance of nature. In most other countries and civilizations these forces, although worshipped as entities in themselves, were soon subsumed under a pantheon of deities, and further, into monotheism. But in China, the forces of nature remained as spiritual entities and also as representations of the heaven above. The inherent balance in nature was eventually defined as Yin and Yang, the feminine/masculine, dark/light, passive/active, rest/movement. This concept of Yin/Yang came to define both the Tao and, later, certain aspects of Neo-Confucianism.

There are two further themes which run through Chinese religions. The first is the mandate for rule in the Chinese Empire, the Middle Kingdom. The emperor rules by t'ien ming, the Will of Heaven. This is not a divine right as is understood in the West, it is more an acquiesence of heaven that the emperor has a mandate. But if the emperor and his dealings should become selfish, arrogant, brutal, then t'ien ming decrees that a new ruler should be found. Therefore it behoves the ruler to behave with concern for his people. And concern for the people is the second of the underlying themes of the religions of China, particularly as expressed by Confucius.

Confucius lived in the last stages of the Chou dynasty, when its rule was enfeebled and lesser rulers were beginning to fight to succeed. It was the period known as the Warring States (c.450–221 BCE), when anarchy and lack of moral standards prompted the formulation of Confucian philosophy. Lao Tzu is supposed to have lived during this same period when Taoism also rose as a recognizable philosophy. It was based partly on all the magical and shamanistic elements of the Shang dynasty and partly on the Yin/Yang balance of everything in the universe.

By the time the first Han dynasty (206–20 CE) came to power, the ethic of Confucius was the means by which the emperor governed and the name, Taoism, was used for the mystical Way that followed the precepts of balance and harmony in all things. Both paths were to exist, side by side and intertwined, for over two thousand years. It may seem at first sight that the two are polar opposites, and academically speaking, that may be so. But the Chinese never made much of a distinction between the philosophical and the religious, between teachers and the great traditions of the teachers, and the way they are practised by the people. Each side – the ethical thought of the Confucian and the understanding of the Taoist – contributes to making up the whole.

Buddhism arrived in the second century CE with its established dogma, canon and ritual well-organized. Both Confucianism and Taoism were obliged to re-examine the forces which drove them. Neo-Confucianism borrowed much from Buddhist philosophy, and so predicated a philosophy of its own in order to compete. Taoism, which had already laid a religious element over the mystical, put out a whole canon of scriptures, and built temples and monasteries.

Eventually, of course, over a thousand years later, around 1400 CE, the three religions were regarded as one, even though they retained their salient identities. It was not thought strange to be a Buddhist, a Taoist and a Confucian at one and the same time, a Chinese synthesis of quietness, meditation and fellow concern.

CONFUCIANISM

To understand Confucianism in any sense you have to realize that it is not strictly a religion – although it became one. But if religion may be defined as a code of values, as a moral stance, as a method of living one's life, here and now (as opposed to any afterlife) to the fullest, then it most certainly is a religion. It has a strong doctrine, a formal canon of writings, involves ritual and, although there are no gods, it has a deep morality. People believed in the strong moral code as laid down by Kung Fu-Tzu, known to the West as Confucius.

Confucius lived in a time of great upheaval, violence and misery under the decadent, unjust and feeble Chou dynasty. The feudal landlords and princes were warring with one another in the attempt to control the Empire. Various proponents of different schools of thought believed that by following their particular precepts, peace and harmony in government would be restored. These various rival schools fell into two categories; those that insisted that a religious or mystical attitude should be the foremost principle, and those that were concerned with life in the day-to-day, eschewing any spiritual dimension.

The mystical element was composed of the Taoists, who stood for spontaneity, nature and the Way, and the Mohists who believed that universal and unconditional love was the answer. These two schools eventually melded to become religious Taoism.

The practical paths were: the Legalists, who propounded rule by strict law and a harsh penal code; the Logicians, who considered the answer lay in agnostic and secular analysis; and the school to which Confucius subscribed, which espoused a return to the moral standards of the ancients. These three philosophies fused and became known as Confucianism.

But interestingly, the Chinese word for Confucianism is Ju, which roughly translated means scholars or literati.

Philosophy is *chia* in Chinese, so one might expect Confucianism to be known as *Ju-chia*. But it is known as *Ju-chiao*, or sometimes *Kung-chiao* or *Li-chiao*, and *chiao* stands for religious teachings. The Chinese do not much discriminate between the two, regarding them as different aspects of the Ultimate Way.

CONFUCIUS AND HIS TEACHINGS

Confucius (551–479 BCE) came from a poor but noble family and was an official in the state of Lu. He admits that he was not an original thinker, but a disseminator of original knowledge; he was not a founder but a restorer of that which was and should be. He was neither agnostic nor sceptic. He believed in the Tao, the Way, and that if there was a god. He had a sense of 'concern' for his peoples, for their well-being and happiness. But he considered that a belief in God was one thing, the other was that one had to live in the world. To this end he devised his code of ethics and morals.

Confucius resigned from being an official in the state of Lu and travelled, hoping to find a ruler willing to govern according to his ancient rules. He found little acceptance from the various warring feudal rulers during his lifetime, but did gather enough converts to his way of thinking and his notional reforms of government.

His basic precept was that 'you should not do unto others that which you would not want done unto you'; that the basis of all social order is *li* – a respect for rights of propriety and convention. He extended the notion of li from being merely the rules of proper conduct and ritual into something deeper – the attitude with which these rules and rituals were conducted, one of respect. It was through this utmost respect when conducting all areas of your life that harmony with the Tao would be achieved. He advocated a meritocracy, whereby a gentleman was not an accident of birth, but could be made by diligence, study, intellect, honesty and righteousness. He believed that governments should rule according to the ancient Way, the Tao; not by the use and abuse of power but with a sense of moral responsibility. That same responsibility, that benign concern that God feels for all his peoples, should be the fundamental concern of the emperors.

CONFUCIAN BELIEFS

The Five Virtues

There are five Virtues in Confucianism which, if followed assiduously, lead to the Way of Heaven. This is less a religious concept than the embracing of a total way of life. Failing in these virtues is shaming, rather than sinful. There is not the Western concept of sin in Confucianism. Shame – even if you are the only one who knows where you have defaulted – is the greater deterrent.

Of these virtues, Jen (benevolence) is the most important. But benevolence scarcely explains it. In the Analects Confucius wrote: 'Jen ... is politeness, liberality, good faith, diligence, generosity.' And not doing to others what you do not like yourself. Mencius (?371–?289 BCE) extended the notion of Jen to a 'disinterested concern' and the Neo-Confucians took it as altruistic love, but falling short of the universal and indiscriminate love of the Mohists. Perhaps Jen might be translated as the ultimate in humanity.

Li (manners) is the next most important virtue. This is respect for others, polite behaviour, both inner as well as outer. But it also includes all aspects – and therefore rites – of ritual and custom, from the etiquette of table manners up to the sacrifices made to heaven. There are three thousand minor and three hundred major rules of li. Following these correctly leads to the desired transformation into sagehood. For a government, the correct procedures of ritual and manners were important to the keeping and ordering of a peaceful society.

Yi is duty. Duty is following prescribed actions. Duty is also righteousness and honesty. Duty also covers the sense of shame.

Chih (wisdom) covers practical as well as moral knowledge, and one should be well grounded in both aspects. Only thus may one tell right from wrong. But it is still morality which is the most important.

Finally, Hsin which is good faith. This implies being trustworthy and keeping promises.

Destiny and Free Will

Confucians hold that man is composed of both elements of destiny and free will and that there is no conflict between them. This is largely due to the acceptance of the Yin/Yang, the opposites which bind and without which the universe cannot exist. It is up to man whether he follows the correct path of jen and li – he may make that choice. But it is up to heaven how long is a life, or whether riches and rewards, material or immaterial, will accrue as a result of a life lived properly. Neither is there any concept of rewards in the afterlife. A Confucian is concerned with the here and now, of living in the world, of achieving the highest condition – that of sagehood. The afterlife is left to the Buddhists and – more or less – to the Taoists.

Life after Death

Although the Chinese have an innate belief in spirits – spirits are in everything – Confucianism has little truck with spirits. They are of the afterlife, and Confucians hold that all consciousness stops at death. Why then, Confucius was asked, go on worshipping ancestors and sacrificing to spirits? Because one owes duty to one's forbears. Ancestors should not be neglected. It was not the sacrifice that was important, it was the sincerity with which any ceremony was performed which was the ultimate in good behaviour.

They admitted to ghosts (because ghosts are mentioned in the Classics), and explained them by saying that if a man died before he was due, then his spirit was likely to roam as a ghost. But the proper way for a spirit to behave was to disperse when the body died. If a ghost appeared at any ceremony of ancestor worship, it was the duty of the spirit to reassemble himself to fulfil his part in duty.

This concept of the duty of the living toward the dead was the Confucians' only concession to the notion of life after death. They rejected both the Buddhist creed of reward and punishment after death and the Taoist ideal of personal immortality. The first they regarded as being too self-interested to have a true morality and the second as ignoring the natural cycle of changes – such as the simple precept of death following life. In the third-century tract, the Chia yu, Confucius is attributed to have said:

> If I say that the dead have consciousness, I am afraid that filial sons and obedient grandsons will burden their lives in order to send off the dead. If I say they have not, then I am afraid that unfilial sons will abandon their parents and refuse to bury them. Do not ask to know whether the dead have consciousness or not. There is no urgency at present, and afterwards you will know for yourself.

If nothing else, Confucianism makes a plea for living in the world.

CONFUCIAN SCRIPTURES

Disciples were aided in spreading Confucianism by the doctrine contained in the Four Books. The first, much of which is in his own words, containing his teachings and how to apply them individually, is the Lun Yu, known as The Analects. The other three may contain some of his writings but are more likely to be disseminations of his code. They are:

The Chung Yung, the Doctrine of the Mean – that man should tread a middle path, neither too passive nor too active, neither too abstinent nor too greedy, that man should strive for the union of order and harmony as the ideal path in life.

The Ta Hsueh, the Book of Great Learning, which applies itself to the principle that only by learning, knowledge, purity of heart and conformity to the Universal Code do you gain perfection.

The Book of Meng Tzu, written by Meng Tzu (also known as

Mencius), who was born roughly a hundred years after the death of Confucius. Meng Tzu most closely epitomizes Confucius's teachings, which were based on the Confucian values of the true gentleman: jen, goodness and benevolence; i, the practice of honesty and righteousness, being attentive and generous; chong, being true to one's own nature; chu, applying the same principles when dealing with others; and hsaio, the notion of obedience and filial piety, which last is a concept that stretches through into every social area of life.

Tradition has it that Confucius also wrote the Five Classics, and he may well have written or annotated part of them but the whole as it stands today was collated over 1600 years after his death by Chu Hsi, during the Sung Dynasty (1130–1200 CE). The Five Classics are:

The Su Ching (the Book of History), purported to be a collection of historical documents going as far back as the legendary ruler Yao and up to the Chou dynasty – although much of it comes from the Later Han dynasty (23–220 CE)

The I Ching (the Book of Changes), is a book of divination. It contains sixty-four hexagrams of six lines each, composed of a variation of broken and unbroken lines, representing the Yin and Yang, the two basic forces of society and nature. The philosophical appendices are supposed to have been the work of Confucius.

The Shi Ching (the Book of Odes), songs and poems to which are attributed highly spiritual meanings.

The Li Ching (the Book of Rites), a collection of the rites to be used in daily life.

The Ch'un Ch'iu (the Annals of Spring and Autumn), a part history of the State of Lu, much of which is said to be by Confucius himself.

The Development of Confucianism

Confucius was the originator of this system of ethical life, belief and administration, and Mencius carried it further, refined it and introduced the mystical element of good versus evil. Whereas Confucius had been involved with outward form, conducted with inner propriety and proper attitude, he refused to address any problem or conflict of inherent good or evil in the nature of man. Mencius, on the other hand, was happy to discuss the issue. He believed in the innate goodness of man, but that it must be prompted, guided and educated to make the fullest use of this goodness.

The third propagator in the early years was Hsun Tzu (300–230 BCE). He was more of a rationalist than Confucius and believed in the inherent evil nature of man, who must be restrained and subjected to severe moral training. Hsun Tzu was out of step with most Confucian philosophers and teachers in this respect. It is understandable, however, that he was inclined toward this train of thought. The China in which he lived was even more lawless and violent than it had been two centuries earlier during Confucius's life.

Neo-Confucianism

Between the early period and the later, Neo-Confucian, period which began c.1000 CE during the Sung dynasty, China saw not only the rise of Taoism as a religious rather than just a spiritual force, but also the advent of Buddhism. Philosophers who felt that the inherent nature of the Chinese people was being subsumed and taken over by matters more to do with the next world than the one they were living in, retaliated and re-examined the thoughts and teachings of Master Kung.

Confucianism had a difficult time during the first millennium of the Buddhist advent in China. It lacked philosophical depth and mystical appeal, particularly in comparison to the wonderful complexities of Buddhism. But in 630 CE the Emperor T'ai Tsung ordered that each prefecture should build a Confucian temple to reverence Confucius the man. This heralded the rise of Confucianism as a religion, not just as a moral ethic.

The religious aspect was followed by philosophical underpinnings which came via Chou Lien-chi from his notion of the Great Ultimate – T'ai-chi – the first principle. It was he, too, who developed the animist theory of Yin and Yang, the two eternal opposites, into an acceptable concept for Confucianism.

There were many contributors to the rediscovery of the principles of Confucianism. It was felt that the well-ordered, cogent philosophers of Buddhism were more than a match for what had become by now rather woolly thinking based on 'things as they had always been'. And because tradition is incredibly important in China, many of them were concerned to return to the Classics and deliver a tighter, more coherent philosophy based on the Confucian ethics.

CONFUCIANISM TODAY

Although it is a philosophical school, and although one can agree with the principles of Confucianism, it is nevertheless a way of life. And one that can be practised only within 'traditional Chinese society'. The leisured intelligentsia does not exist any more to continue its practice. After two thousand years of reasonably benevolent rule and of co-existing with the mystical Tao, Confucianism had grown stagnant – so entrenched in bureaucracy that it was impervious to change. The complacent and arrogant ruler and his bureaucrats scorned and dismissed the danger of sea attacks from Western powers. Nor was the seriousness of internal attacks recognized until it was far too late.

The first of these came from Hung Hsiu Ch'ii (1813–64) who harnessed popular dissatisfaction into an army which was successful in overthrowing the governance of one state for eleven years. The second came from Mao Tse-tung (1893–1976), who used the techniques of the West and the inbuilt internal Confucian morals (including that of changing the ruler) to effect his own religion. Confucianism may be dead as a way of life in China, but Confucius's wisdom lives on in his philosophy and his teachings.

TAOISM

The Tao is the Way. It was and is for ever. It is anarchy. It is natural. It is spontaneous. It is mystical. It is poetic. It is emptiness. It is eternal and unchanging.

But what *is* the Tao?

The Tao is the foundation of all being. Its indefinability is part of its essence; exemplified in the first chapter of one of the seminal books of mystical Taoism, the Tao te Ching:

> The Tao that can be told is not the eternal Tao.
> The Name that can be named is not the eternal name.
> The nameless is the beginning of heaven and earth.
> The named is the mother of ten thousand things.
> Ever desireless, one can see the mystery.
> Ever desiring, one can see the world made manifest.
> These two spring from the same source but differ in name:
>   this appears as darkness.
> Darkness within darkness.
> The gate to all mystery.

THE WAY OF THE TAO

Taoism stems, in part, from the earlier shamanic-magical religion that was prevalent during the Shang dynasty (1766–1122 BCE). Then scholars during the Chou dynasty in the sixth century BCE were the first to formulate the concept of Yin and Yang, the feminine/masculine, as part of the 'scientific' view of the universe. The Yin/Yang, the fundamental power of opposites, is a quality that permeates the Tao. Taoism has a deep alliance with the essence of nature. Another strand of this mystical philosophy comes from a deeper and darker primeval age of belief in ancient goddesses. The Tao te Ching says:

> The valley spirit never dies;
> It is the woman, primal mother.

Her gateway is the root of heaven and earth
Heaven and earth last for ever.
Why do heaven and earth last forever?
They are unborn
So ever living.

When the goddess gave birth it was considered to be the transition from the state of not-being (wu) into the state of being (yu). Therefore everything which lives comes from that nothingness which is not-being and will eventually return to that same nothingness. And eventually the goddess was replaced with a concept, an absolute that was stillness incarnate, yet ever moving and creating.

This is the paradox of the Tao, the opposites which do not exist without each other, because without knowing one opposite, the other cannot be discerned. There is no movement without stillness, no ugliness without beauty, no emptiness without fullness – and in this last, even emptiness is not necessarily empty, given its latent capacity, like a bowl, to be filled. This capacity is the te, Virtue, the magical, mysterious energy which defines the actions within the non-actions of the Tao. It is the te which binds the Tao to all things, which manifests the Tao as the One. The Tao gave birth to T'ai-chi, immortal breath, T'ai-chi gave birth to the Yin and Yang, the eternal opposites, which also contain within them the seeds of their opposite; they gave birth to Water, Earth and Heaven, and these three gave birth to the myriad things of the universe. Chapter 41 of the Tao te Ching states:

The Tao gave birth to One.
The One gave birth to Two.
The Two gave birth to the Three
And the Three gave birth to the ten thousand things.

Therefore the One is not only part of but also the direct antithesis of the Tao. And the wholeness of the One is in everything and at the same time both ultimate and relative. This is the fundamental doctrine of Taoism.

The essence of the Yin/Yang duality is what drives the cycles of changes, such as autumn into winter and so round the seasons. Within that change, however, is the unpredictable: snowflakes all of a different pattern, falling leaves on the earth. Taoists contemplate change and understand the necessity; decay and death being as important a part of the whole as renewal, birth and life. Things are as they are, and if the unexpected arrives – well, so be it. Sometimes you can influence the change within the change, sometimes not. This contemplation leads to tranquillity and stillness.

From the interaction of the Yin and Yang come the Five Elements, or Activities: the wu hsing. The doctrine of wu hsing is later than that of Yin/Yang, but developed from it. The Two become the Five, five elements – wood, fire, metal, water and earth – that make up the material world. Sometimes they are represented as colours, blue (or green), red, yellow, white and black because their activities, and functions, are as much allegorical as physical. For the Taoist, contemplation of these Five Activities sheds light on the near mystery of nature's workings, inculcating a reverence for the mystery. On a level of more mundane understanding, some Taoists have used their knowledge of the Yin/Yang, Five Element continuum of change to become involved in earthly divination and possible manipulation of ensuing events. The adept, however, wishes merely to remark without interference, in silence and tranquillity.

On a more elevated level, the pure Yin of earth meets the pure Yang of heaven in what are called 'dragon veins'. The closest analogy is that of the bodily meridians that are inherent in yoga and acupuncture. The 'dragon veins' link the earth to the sky, and are the channels for the yan ch'i (the breath of heaven) and the yin ch'i (the breath of earth) to meet and mingle. Much Chinese painting expresses these psychic channels, sometimes leading to that flash of insight where, for a moment, the viewer (beholder) is taken to the realm where all things are made clear. In this there is much resemblance to Zen Buddhism. These 'dragon veins' were also instrumental in the development of the science of Feng Shui, the art of geomancy: siting buildings, graves, etc., where they have the most harmonious interaction between Yin and Yang.

There are three further concepts, known as the Three Treasures, which are of importance in the Taoist canon of belief. They are: ching (essence), ch'i (vitality) and shen (Spirit), all essentials in yogic use. They are also living forces in every level of being from the smallest to the largest. The yogis combine these forces in various different ways to achieve the ideal of the Supreme State of Being.

It was an alchemy of mind and body, of refining both to achieve at the very least longevity, and (they thought it quite possible) immortality. And the early sages thought that ultimate refinement of the body through the use of wai tan (the external elixir of chemicals, drugs and metals) and the corresponding refinement of both body and mind through nei tan (the inner elixir of controlling the ching, ch'i and shen) would without doubt lead to the Life Forever.

Many followers of the Way misread the early texts and, not understanding their true spiritual import, thought that these forces were external, magical, and were the alchemical process that turns lead into gold. Many would-be Taoists became literally magicians and alchemists, concerned with the practical application of extracting gold from baser stuff. It laid a patina of populism over the ungraspable elements of the Tao quest.

> Man follows the earth.
> Earth follows the heaven.
> Heaven follows the Tao.
> Tao follows what is natural.

> Tao te Ching, XXV

A true Taoist lives as close to an accord with nature as possible. This is because there is a Tao of Heaven, a Tao of Earth and a Tao of Man. In the earliest days, the Tao of Man was one and the same as the Tao of Nature, and life was lived without battling against the vagaries. This comes back to the acceptance of cycles and change. The total acceptance of what the natural life – complete with upheavals – induces a serenity, a carelessness. This is the course of wu wei (no action) but not in the sense of a stolid block of wood, doing nothing: wu wei is the action of going with the flow, of acceptance.

Yield and overcome;
Bend and be straight;
Empty and be full;
Wear out and be new;
Be really whole,
And all things will come to you.

Tao te Ching, XXII

And

The softest thing in the universe
Overcomes the hardest thing in the universe.
That without substance can enter where there is no room.
Hence I know the value of non-action.

Ibid, XLIII

Stillness. All activity should be balanced with a period of quietude. And this quietude, this stillness, should be of first the body and then the mind. The mind should 'contemplate the inner radiance'. The idea is to transcend the darker forces of all passions, but not to give in, either, to the gluttony of pleasures. Excess at either end of the scale is against stillness, is departing from the Tao. By turning from it, stillness is born, through stillness one may turn away. Eventually stillness brings internal joy and 'ever-increasing joy in stillness'.

The Goals of the Way

Firstly, to be in harmony with nature, to live by its rules, to enjoy happiness here and now, without regard for the future. Secondly, while you live by these rules, and acquire the inner stillness, your spirit gradually becomes more and more refined. Then, finally, after your body, the spirit's housing, falls away with death, your spirit is free to merge with the Spirit of the Ultimate Tao. In other words, to become immortal.

The ultimate of being on the path of the Tao is to achieve perfection in a Supreme State of Being. This state is impersonal, exalted, and above everything else. Taoists do not believe in One God. The Supreme State of Being is above gods (whom they consider to be in need of further instruction, being as yet imperfect, if useful). Merging with the undifferentiated Tao is a divinity more divine than any Divine.

Ritual

Modern-day rituals, as practised among the Chinese diaspora, are based on the Yin/Yang five element activities. A candle is lit, representing the T'ai-chi, the primordial breath, the head of mankind. This candle lights two others for the Yang and Yin: one for the soul in the heart of man and the other for the essence in the belly, the intuitive level. These three candles also represent the Three Spirits of the Transcendent Tao who govern heaven, earth and water. This ritual of lighting the candles operates on three levels: the macrocosmic in heaven, earth and water; the microcosmic, in the intellect, love and intuition of man, and, finally, on the spiritual level, in that the Tao is ever-present and working.

The Five Element ritual (known as su-ch'i) takes place around the winter solstice and is the Chiao festival of renewal. It involves taking the five elements, represented by talismans drawn on coloured silks, and placing them in baskets of rice. This symbolizes renewal of the five elements and of the eternal round of new life, maturity, harvest and security throughout the seasons. This is followed by a prayer.

On the last day of the Chiao festival, the Taoist priest takes the five elements from the rice, and 'ingests' them into his body, meditatively, to correspond with the five organs. The people can see demonstrated through ritual the mystical union with the Tao.

THE TAOIST SCRIPTURES

The essence of mystical Taoism is found in the Tao te Ching and the book of Chuang Tzu. The Tao te Ching is purported to have been written by Lao Tzu, a philosopher said to have lived for up to 200 years around the sixth century BCE. It dates mostly from the third century BCE although some verses are older, and may have been penned by Lao Tzu – if he existed.

He came to be revered as part of the Taoist pantheon – when it was developed some centuries later. The Tao te Ching is really the only well-known book on early Taoist thought and application. It was directed at the sage-ruler, and informs him that only by becoming one with the Tao; by acting like soft water, adaptable and bending; by returning to a childlike state, and following the harmony of wu wei, the abstaining from volitional activity, will he achieve the tranquillity needed to be the sage and wise ruler of his intention.

The next most famous book of the Taoist canon is the Chuang Tzu by the philosopher of the same name. It is probable that only the first seven chapters are by him, the rest by others of similar thinking. It leans more to a sense of the personal than the Tao te Ching, of the embrace of Taoism for the ordinary person – in fact it is suggested that if one is a true follower of the Way, through wu wei and tzu-jan (naturalness), then ruling anything is out of the question. Chuang Tzu talks of immortality, in the spiritual sense, to which end he suggests certain breathing exercises. These were taken later as models in the Taoist search for physical immortality. Various ascetic disciplines, such as meditation and concentration are advocated in order to achieve that sense of emptiness the Tao expresses – the 'treasure house of Heaven. Pour into it, and it will never be filled; pour out of it, and it will never be emptied ... This is called the hidden light.' Another chapter urges the acceptance of change and fluctuation as the natural order of things. This premise allowed Mao Tse-tung to harness the energies of a Chinese people who had an innate understanding of the virtues of upheaval and change.

The bulk of the Taoist canon, the Tao-tzang, was written down during the Sung dynasty (960–1279 CE), a period of great artistic and philosophical flowering. But it was not printed in its totality until 1436. It consisted, originally, of 1,464 works arranged, in emulation of the Buddhist Tripitaka writings, in three sections. But much of it was destroyed and it now consists of 1,120 works arranged in a different fashion.

Even so, it is considered that the present arrangement dates from the fourth and fifth centuries CE: it is divided into the San Tung (Three Vaults) and Ssu Fu (Four Supplements). The first of the Three Vaults is the Tung Chen (True Vault) which is focused on the ritual texts and meditatory practices of the Highest Pure sect of Mao Shan. The second, the Tung Hsuan (Mysterious Vault), contains more ritual and the texts of the Sacred Jewel sect. The third is the Tung Shen (Spirits Vault) which is about the spirits that the nominal founder of the Heavenly Master sect Chang Tao-ling discovered.

The Ssu Fu contains writings from an earlier period, including the Tao te Ching and the Chuang Tzu, many other philosophical texts such as the T'ai Ping Ching (Classic of Great Peace) and various treatises on alchemy, both internal and external.

There is one other book, the I Ching, the Classic of Changes. The I Ching is part of the Confucian canon, but as it was also used extensively by Taoists, it could be thought of as part of the Chinese spiritual canon. It is the book of the Wu Hsing Five Activities. Meditation on the 64 hexagrams (each a various combination of Yin and Yang) brings about understanding of the nature of cycles and change.

THE TAOIST PANTHEON

The philosophy of the early Taoists was intended not only as a path for personal salvation but as a 'right' way for rulers to govern their people. But as Confucianism gained the upper hand in the courts, certain aspects of Taoism began to appeal more to the lowlier members of society. In the first two centuries CE, Taoism diverged, on the one hand, into the mystical and alchemical, and, on the other, into the religious.

The religious movement was founded, effectively, by Chang Tao-ling (c.150 CE). It embodied much of the shamanism of earlier times, and its hereditary rulers used magic ritual, exorcism and charms to keep demons and ghosts at bay and ensure the well-being of their followers. A whole pantheon of gods came into being, as manifestations of the One, the emanation of the unknowable Tao. The first was called Yuan-shih t'ien-tsun, Heavenly Elder of the Mysterious Origin. He was enlarged into a trinity which may be taken as a cosmological example of how the Tao came into being in three stages. This included T'ai-lao Tao-Chun (the August Ruler of the Tao) and T'ai-shang Lao-chun (August Old Ruler) who supposedly is Lao Tzu himself. During the early part of Sung dynasty (960–1126 CE), Yuan-shih t'ien-tsun became known as Yu-Huang, Jade Emperor Lord on High. Giving the gods a bureaucracy that imitated the courts of the rulers, the notion of heaven became accessible to the ordinary person.

There is a plethora of gods in the Chinese pantheon, all with their own offices – such as the Ministries of Thunder, Healing, Fire, Epidemics. There are the gods of the city and of the hearth, of happiness, longevity and wealth. Many of these still have homage paid to them today.

THE HISTORY OF TAOISM

Sects appeared, most of which were concerned with earlier elements of shamanism, and whose rituals against demons and ghosts were fairly crude. In particular the leaders of the T'ai p'ing (Universal Peace) sect, which combined Mohism with Taoism, used magic to see their followers through difficulties.

One early leader of the T'ai p'ing sect, Chang Chio, claimed that sin was the root of all ills. He believed in the ultimate efficacy of private and public confession as the first step to salvation, after which the aspirant was given divine protection through the medium of a drink of water which had been blessed. If ills befell him thereafter, either he had not confessed his sins thoroughly, or he did not believe fervently enough. Chang Chio instigated a Taoist rebellion in 184 CE in response to appalling social and economic conditions. Until the nineteenth century and the rebellion of Hung Hsiu-chu'an against the Manchus and the Opium Wars, it was the biggest Taoist rebellion and lasted several years.

Another movement, founded by Chang Tao-ling (probably in the first century CE), was originally based on his supposed magical powers. This movement became hereditary and was known as the Taoism of the Celestial Master. But the cruder populistic practices of this group were anathema to philosophical Taoists.

The rise of Buddhism, with its ethical and moral structure and its particular philosophy, was a threat to the sway that the Taoists had held up till then. K'ou Ch'ien-chih (c.415 CE) purged the rituals of Taoism of some of the excesses and declared that the doctrine of suffering as posited by the Buddhists was unnatural in comparison to the naturalness of following the Way. And the Way was to be found in moral conduct.

Monastic life emerged during the T'ang dynasty (618–906 CE) for the first time. For the layman, Taoism took on a puritanical bent and began to be perceived as more rigorous than Buddhism. During the following Sung dynasty Taoism began to dissipate and be absorbed into various Buddhists creeds, and into Neo-Confucianism. By now, few of the intelligentsia in China believed in the possibility of ultimate immortality, even though many of them still went through the practices of it, and much of the feeling that informs Taoism went into paintings and poetry instead. Other practitioners of the art of immortality became hermits, subscribing to the original notion that Taoism is personal.

Much of it went underground into various sects and cults. Some were localized, based on popular superstitious Taoism, and were outlawed more often than not. Their resemblance to formal and pure Taoism lay in their anarchy. Wherever they were, they were a threat to the ruling bureaucracy and occasionally erupted in rebellions. By the end of the thirteenth century there were two distinct Taoisms: of the North and the South. The northern sect was called Chuan-chen, Perfecting the True. More ascetic than most Taoist movements, it posited tranquillity and harmony with nature. In the South the Celestial Master held sway. The Cheng-i (Principle One) sect used magic and charms against evil spirits, and acted as mediums. But, in fact, their reputation was so great that these sorcerers were often summoned to court to deal with various natural disasters – and were rewarded for their efforts. Even though their aims seemed to be radically different, most sects managed both to tolerate and cooperate with each other, particularly against foreign threats of force.

Many sects survived political oppression, for instance under the Manchu dynasty (1644–1911), and the onset of Communism under Mao Tse-tung, precisely because of the underlying anarchy of the Tao. And Mao Tse-tung harnessed this anarchy.

TAOISM TODAY

Most Chinese people are a mixture of all the main themes of the Chinese religions. Over the centuries Taoism has taken from Buddhism and Confucianism, and vice versa, so that in some areas they are barely distinguishable. If there is a future for Taoism, in China or elsewhere, it probably lies more with the spiritual and mystical elements than with the ritual. Taoism has survived – because of its anarchy and its sense of freedom, its expression in art and poetry, and also because to live in harmony with the cycles of life is to live in harmony with the Tao.

BUDDHISM

The acceptance of Buddhism in China began in the second century CE with the expansion of the trade routes and much cultural cross-fertilization between China and other countries, particularly India. China is the only country into which Buddhism has penetrated to have had a clearly defined culture and religion already in place, which makes its conversion to Buddhism quite remarkable. It also says a great deal for the adaptability of Buddhism, in that it absorbed much local custom. By the sixth century CE the domination of Buddhism in China was complete.

BUDDHISM IN CHINA

An astonishing number of Buddhist sects proliferated in China, all based on a particular sutra – an authoritative text claimed to have been spoken by the Buddha. Each sect took a different aspect of the Dharma as expressed in their favourite sutra, therefore every time a new preacher appeared he gained adherents, bringing in another school of thought that neither absorbed nor superimposed on those gone before. Most of them did not survive their original masters, or, if they did, not for long. There are five main schools whose teachings survive – either more or less in their original form, if not in their original country, or by having such a great influence that there was no need to maintain a separate tradition.

The first two, T'ien-t'ai and Hua-yen, both sought to absorb and harmonize. T'ien-t'ai was established by Chih-i (538–97 CE), as an intellectual school, placing great emphasis on traditional meditation. It posited a hierarchy, not only of people, but also a plurality of levels of both thought and attainment. Its most important scripture is the Lotus Sutra, which is regarded as perfection. T'ien-t'ai became Tendai in Japan.

The Hua-yen school was based on the Avatamsaka Sutra — a philosophy of totality, in which it is recognized that everything is (harmoniously) related to everything else, that everything is contained in everything else. Again it was highly intellectual, but unlike T'ien-t'ai it did not last as a school, only as an influence in China. In Japan it became the Kegon sect.

The third school, Chen-yen, was based on Mantrayana Buddhism. It took as its scriptures the Mahavairocana and the Vajrasekhara Sutras. Full of ritual, it uses mantra, mudra and mandala (symbolizing speech, body and thought) and a complicated cosmology that is understood only by the initiate. It transferred successfully to Japan as the Shingon sect. (Recently, apparently, it has been reintroduced into China with some success.)

The last two sects, the Pure Land and the Ch'an sects, are exclusive, rather than harmonizing. They demand total adherence of the follower to their singular paths, and there is only one point of contact between them. Both are proponents of sudden, rather than gradual, enlightenment. Otherwise their differences are pronounced.

The Pure Land school is dedicated to meditation on the figure of the Amitabha Buddha in his Pure Land of Sukhavati (the 'Land of Happiness', or the Mahayana nirvana). The practice involved reciting the name of Amitabha over and over, in order to reach a state of grace. Because of its utter simplicity it attracted adherents of all sorts. Its basis is the Amitabha Sutra, and commentaries on the Sutra. Pure Land, with its emphasis on divine help in order to achieve realization, is far removed from the original teachings, but under the eclectic umbrella of Buddhism it does not matter.

The Ch'an school differs in almost every degree. It is mystical and insightful. There are no scriptures, transmission is through the mind, master to pupil. It emphasizes spontaneity and iconoclasm to break down the barriers to enlightenment. It offers no routine practice — adherence to routine is as binding as desire. The influence of Taoism is much discerned in its teachings. It is best known in its Japanese incarnation as Zen.

Buddhism in China has gone through various divergences and syncretisms. Overall it has been a remarkable success. This is due not only to its above-mentioned adaptability but also to the devotion and viability of the Sangha. Each monk and nun was received into Buddhism, rather than into one of the proliferating sects. They provided a steady foundation, ensuring that Buddhism – in spite of occasional, and sometimes lengthy, persecutions – remained alive. The state, although remaining secular, always supported the Sangha until the advent of Communism when the work ethic became paramount. This, inevitably, destroyed much spiritual practice. Previous pogroms destroyed temple and art, but it was relatively easy to rebuild and renew when the Sangha remained strong. Now, the cultural usefulness of temple and art is recognized, but the Sangha are finding their support less secure. Spiritual discipline in China is now permitted, even if it is not encouraged. There is a long way to go before one may be sure of its survival there but, if any religion is to survive in China, it will be Buddhism.

RELIGIONS IN JAPAN: SHINTO

Sometimes a religion may be defined as much by geography, geology and the people who inhabit the landscape as it is by doctrine, ritual or belief. The myths of early Shinto, the indigenous Japanese religion and way of life, reflect the mountains and rivers of Japan and the awe of and closeness to nature of its peoples. It may be construed as broadly animist and reflecting both the chaos and the order of the natural world.

The creation stories, as written in the Nihon Shoki ('The Written Chronicles of Japan'), reflect the magical qualities of the whole Japanese archipelago. They also reflect the three main themes that have run through Shinto since its earliest times.

Worship of and sacrifice to the kami is the first. The kami are the mysterious forces of nature associated primarily with permanent topographical features, especially unusual mountains (Sacred Mountains), rocky cliffs, caves, springs, trees and stones. Many folk tales emanate from these places – they often refer to animal possession, chiefly involving foxes, raccoon-dogs, badgers, dogs and cats bewitching people, more often women than men. Celestial bodies play only incidental roles as kami, but the spirits are present in everything – nature, ideas, ancestors, famous people. Worship of the kami, in all their various forms, is what united not only the separate localities, but also the country under the rule of the Emperor.

The second theme that has run throughout the history of Shinto is that the Emperor is divine, although his divinity, popularity and influence have waxed and waned over the centuries. The third theme is ritual purification from every sort of pollution.

THE MYTH OF ORIGINS

Writings

As a set of prehistoric agricultural ceremonies, Shinto was never endowed with a supporting body of philosophical literature – although there is written mythology, laws governing the indigenous religion, and procedures for Shinto shrine ceremonies and for the administrative structure concerning shrines and ceremonies. There are two particular books: Kojiki (Records of Ancient Matters) and the Nihongi or Nihon Shoki (Chronicles of Japan). Both contain descriptions of rulers' lives, history of ceremonies and building of shrines, etc, but in particular they contain myths.

In the beginning heaven and earth were not separate. Together they formed the cosmos, a vaguely oval mass of chaos. In time the purer elements of heaven ascended while the baser earth settled below. Eventually a mass of reeds grew between the two, and out of these reeds gods and spirits were formed. Two of them, Izanagi and Izanami, the male and female principles, married and created the four islands of Japan and the other gods and spirits inhabited the rivers, trees rocks, mountains and other physical features of the country. This is the first tenet of Shinto – that all of nature is inhabited by spirits, kami, and for a happy life these spirits must be prayed to and placated.

Izanami died while giving birth to Fire and descended into the underworld. This is the first Death, the first pollution which needed purification. Izanagi followed her but was so disgusted by the filth and putrefaction he found there, he ran away and determined to cleanse himself of any pollution that may have clung to him. Izanagi dived into the sea, and from the cleansing of his right eye came the Goddess of the Sun, Amaterasu; from his left eye, the God of the Moon, Tsukiyomi (of whom very little is heard thereafter); and from his nose sprang Susano-o, the God of the Withering Wind. This cleansing from pollution is one of the central beliefs of Shinto.

The importance of fertility and the evils of pollution is illustrated in a second myth: that of the Rock Cave. The Sun

Goddess, Amaterasu, rules fertility and growth. But the considerable energies of Susano-o, the Withering Wind, are spent in blocking or polluting irrigation channels, laying waste the crops and leaving excrement all over the place. Amaterasu is so revolted by the behaviour of Susano-o that she retreats into a rock cave and refuses to come out. In order to entice her out, the kami dig up a sakaki tree, place a mirror on the top branch, jewels on the middle branches and hang the bottom branches with blue and white strips of material. They also recite hymns of great praise to the deity, of her glory and fruitfulness. Amaterasu is so delighted with the purity and perfection of the prayers and the singing that she comes out, and the way back into the dark cave is blocked.

It is an archetypal description of the eclipse of the sun, the fear it engenders in the population and their intrinsic need to prevent it happening again. How can the day be renewed and the successive seasons roll on without the sun to heat, illumine and fertilize?

This tale highlights a further point; that it is how the prayers are said, how the hymns are sung, how the outward form of devotion is handled, which is most important when addressing the deity. These prayers must not only contain the right sentiments, they must also be spoken in the correct and most beautiful manner. The outward form of prayer was at least, if not more, important than the content. Shinto belief and practice centred solely on outward cleansing from pollution. A heart could be as black as pitch, but if the words were said with precision and beauty, then the supplicant was cleansed. No account was taken of any inner or moral condition, nor was there any ritual for cleansing the inner man.

THE HISTORY OF SHINTO

Early Shinto was concerned with fertility, the sun and with food more than anything else. Shamans (miko) performed the ceremonies to the kami. Eventually those of the Yamato tribe did so on behalf of the other tribes and their chieftain assumed duties that led to the headship of the Shinto state. Shinto became political (Kokutai Shinto) in the eighth century when Yamato writers ascribed divine origins to the imperial family and so claimed legitimacy for rule. As the direct descendant of the Sun Goddess, the Emperor, head of the Shinto state, embodied the spirit of the kami and was infallible. It follows that many birthplaces of such emperors are now shrines. The concept of the Emperor's divinity has fluctuated over the centuries, depending on the status of the Emperor and his powers, peaking in the mid-nineteenth century after seventeenth-century writers espoused a terrific rise of nationalism, morally validated in 1890, in the Imperial Rescript on Education. In 1945 the Emperor finally and publicly renounced his divinity.

With the advent of Buddhism from China in the sixth century CE, Shinto, while still not taking on a very concrete form, began to gain slightly more definition. It gained a name. It was described as The Way of the Gods (Tao Shin in Chinese) or Shinto. And by the time a slightly different Buddhism arrived (less Chinese in character, more adaptable, and therefore more acceptable to the Japanese mind) two centuries later there is evidence that already a degree of syncretism was being practised. The Shinto kami were manifestations of the Buddhist pantheon, and Shinto itself was regarded as the local form of the eternal Buddhist Truth. It was a time of adaptation, of amalgamation; the beginning of what became known as Dual Shinto.

At the same time, the precepts of Confucius started to filter into Japan. It provided a moral backbone for Shinto as a concept for living in the world, and the Confucian stress on loyalty, right behaviour, benevolence, honesty and obedience became part of the samurai canon.

By the time Christianity arrived in 1549, the rule of the Emperor was all but over and Japan was under the rule of the samurai and the shogunate. Buddhism and Shinto had become intertwined over the centuries, much as a result of first one and then the other gaining the upper hand. But although the general instinct of the country was to absorb and amalgamate, there were certain areas that were kept solely for

Shinto devotion. For instance, no Buddhist influence nor building was allowed near the two shrines at Ise and Izumo. Eventually these places were to provide a focus for the new Shinto.

This State Shinto, as it became known, was identified as an obligatory ethic, with the return of the Emperor in the nineteenth century, in 1868. Were it to be classified as a religion, it would be voluntary. The idea was to strip away the appurtenances of Buddhism, Confucianism and even Christianity and leave Shinto in its original purity. By now, of course, the original was all but lost and the Shinto the scholars propounded was really a synthesis and less than pure.

It was decreed that Buddha was, in fact, a manifestation of the Shinto Kami. And the priests rationalized that all the different names and forms of God were in reality the one God. State Shinto was to be a focus for the new imperialism and nationalism that arose in Japan during the years of the last century.

State Shinto had imbibed enough of Buddhist and other tenets never to return to its full and external form of early or folk Shinto. In an attempt to rid Shinto of its overlaid (as they saw it) duality, they created a climate for the rise and growth of Sect Shinto – many of whose branches are, again, a direct synthesis of Shinto, Buddhist and other beliefs.

SHINTO BELIEF AND RITUAL IN EVERYDAY LIFE

Shrines

There are three principal types of shrine in Japan. The most numerous are those dedicated to the local kami, to which people go individually, or as a family, for a variety of reasons – travel, upcoming exams, to give thanks – as well as for the various festivals. The size of the shrine varies, depending on which kami resides there and the purpose of the shrine. The larger ones have an offering house, a hall in which the spirit resides which the worshipper does not enter.

On entering through the gates the supplicant rings a bell to attract the attention of the resident kami. He leaves an offering, but is not permitted to look at the manifestation of the spirit. This representation may be a rock, a jewel, or a relic. The not knowing preserves the numinousness of the kami. Occasionally, however, the object of devotion is some tree or stone.

Shinto shrines are everywhere in Japan and are very noticeable in the landscape. They are frequently red and white, with very distinctive roofs and gates. There are shrines throughout the country that are dedicated to one particular area of life, such as business or study. There are also the great national shrines. Two of the most important are the Ise and Izumo shrines in the southern half of the main island of Honshu – so much so that a daughter of the Imperial family used to be sent as chief priestess. Others include the Meiji shrine in Tokyo, which honours the eponymous Emperor and the Yasakuni shrine, dedicated to the souls of the war dead. Most people hope to pray at them at least once in sixty years. Many shrines are elaborately rebuilt every twenty years at great expense.

Ritual

Ritual is all-important in Shinto. There is little doctrine, and so it is direct experience and communication with the kami and the ritual which pervades an visit to a Shinto temple which drives the belief. Shinto ceremonies (matsuri) are designed to appeal to the kami, for benevolent treatment and protection, and consist of abstinence (imi), offerings, prayers and purification. Community ceremonies take place at fixed times during the year, and visits to Shinto shrines are made at stages marking life's progress.

The order of ritual is a fixed pattern and done with great deliberation. Before entering the shrine itself, the worshipper rinses his hands, face and mouth from the trough of clean water that stands anterior to the shrine. All those who are requesting special blessings are purified by the priests. All participants make obeisances in the direction of the Shintai (the god-body); the door of the inner sanctuary is opened and the little sacrifices of food and drink, plus a branch of the evergreen sakaki tree, are offered. This is followed by prayers, music and dancing after which everything is removed, the shrine door is closed, everyone makes a final obeisance and all go on to eat and drink.

Shinto stresses purity. It is concerned with life and the benefits of this world, because pollution and death are to be avoided at all costs. It is considered that ethically, what is good for the group is morally proper. Aberrations may be erased by purification. Purification procedures make worshippers presentable, and therefore their pleas are acceptable to the kami.

If a would-be worshipper is not clean enough (even after purification by water), to enter the temple and stand before the kami, he might be purified by exorcism (harae). This is the oldest of current Shinto practices, stretching back to the eighth century. It used to be practised twice a year to wash away the influence of Susano-o. Now such ceremonies are performed to negate antisocial behaviour, or to counteract the stigma still attached to certain illnesses and disasters, childbirth, death, and even nightmares or omens. Shinto has always had its superstitious side, which still runs just below the surface. Running water or some other neutralizing agent is preferred, but purification can be achieved by other means, such as making an effigy and disposing of it, or by sprinkling salt (like the great sumo wrestlers before a bout), by taking part in or watching drama in which various baleful spirits are destroyed. Personal abstention (imi) used to be part of the purification ritual but as time went by the honour finally devolved into a practice only for priests.

Festivals

There are a great many festivals (matsuri) in Japan, held for major and minor celebrations. They fall broadly into three categories: ancestral; those of exorcism and purification; and agricultural. Festivals in Japan, whether of Shinto or Buddhist origin, have the welcome effect of uniting the country (or on a smaller level, the locality) with a common cause and are usually well attended.

Matsuri today means the ceremonies of ritual group worship but its deeper meaning is approach and accordance with the Divine. It is a coming together of the Divine and the human, both renewing and affirming their respective lives and energies. The kami is welcomed by the people and treated with great hospitality. If he is pleased his power will increase, which can only be of benefit to the community.

It is to Shinto, rather than to any other of the religions, that the newborn is dedicated. The baby is taken at thirteen days old to the shrine to be placed under the care of the kami. This is reinforced a few years later when both boys of five and girls of three and seven are taken to the shrine on 15 November. Shinto marriages, however, have only been performed since 1901 (before that it was never deemed a religious ceremony), but these tend to take place, not at the shrine, but in some other purpose-built building. They will place an offering at a shrine, though, and receive blessings. Death is under the aegis of the Buddhists – and Shinto is happy to leave it there.

Most of the festivals in Japan are an admixture of all the religions that the country has taken to her heart. But the most important of the national Shinto festivals are at New Year, in spring and autumn. The New Year festival is called Shogatsu. At home the old year is swept away by a thorough cleaning and paying of debts, relatives and friends are visited and the new year is prepared for. Best clothes are worn and special food is prepared and eaten. The 'first' visit to the local shrine is necessary in order to return for burning the amulets and charms from the previous New Year, and also to spend a few moments in quiet contemplation and dedication. Some travel overnight to be at a particular shrine in the early hours, or to make certain they arrive in one of the mountain-top shrines just as the sun is breaking to wash their faces in the enhancing rays of Amaterasu.

Spring and autumn are the times for honouring ancestors and visiting graves. This has taken the place, mostly, of the rituals of welcoming in spring, and the thanking in autumn, of the rice-kami. In Ise, however, there is still a special rice field used for the Ise Divine Rice Planting Ceremony, a rite which is supposed to be over 1,500 years old.

SHINTO TODAY

There is no state religion in Japan. There are, however, quite a few new religions, many based on Buddhism, which seem to be spectacularly successful. It has not followed that Shinto has lost any support. The adherents claimed by each religion outnumbers Japan's total population. This is no statistical cover-up on the part of the various religions, it merely shows that the Japanese are as eclectic in their choice of religion day to day, as they have been over thousands of years of assimilation.

Because it is so old, because it touches on the primitive areas of life, because of its ancient affinity with nature and the rolling seasons, Shinto still appeals to the average Japanese person. It is easy, in Japan, to be involved with many aspects of religious behaviour, both at particular points in life or at the various festivals. The Japanese carry a courtesy and a social obligation that is quite firmly rooted in their oldest religion, and find no problem in following it in spite of increasing secularism.

BUDDHISM

Japan has ever been receptive to outside influence, often embracing new ideas with an alacrity which is astonishing. Yet it has been safe, paradoxically, from outside interference. Before the advent of Buddhism via Korea in the sixth century CE, it was still a relatively primitive country, although already with a strict social hierarchy which owed some of its notions to Confucianism. Buddhism brought art in all its forms to Japan in a high degree and dominated Japanese culture for over ten centuries. It is in Japan that the apogee of Buddhist devotional art is to be found.

By the seventh century Buddhism had become part of the state and for two centuries consolidated itself as the official religion to the extent that all the provinces were obliged to build a temple, house monks and nuns, have a copy of the Prajnaparamit Sutra and a sixteen-foot Buddha image. All the major sects of China were introduced, each in turn was allowed its influence at court.

The Kegon (Hua-yan) sect, in the eighth century, demonstrated full adaptability by recognizing the Emperor's part in its doctrine of totality. The Tendai sect gained ascendancy some 50 years later. Brought to Japan by Dengyo (767–822 CE), it did not lose its intellectual capabilities, but became even more catholic and eclectic in its tastes and teachings. All new sects which appeared some centuries later have their foundations in Tendai, including Nichiren. In spite of its hierarchical leanings (always a popular notion in Japan) it encouraged everyone to follow the path of Buddhahood.

At around the same time, c.806 CE, Kobo (774–835), who had studied the Ch'en-yen teaching, founded the Shingon sect. In Japan, Shingon continued to draw on the Mantrayana philosophies and ceremonies, but was as catholic as Tendai. Indeed, each fed the other, minimizing doctrinal differences over the centuries. Kobo, with his talent for reconciling not only the various streams of Buddhism but Shinto too, played quite a hand in this syncretism.

In the twelfth century Buddhism became the religion of the people, not just that of the rulers at court. Sects proliferated and appealed to those who up till now had been excluded by reason of social hierarchy. By far the most important is the cult of Amida Buddha, the Jodo sect, founded by Honen (1133–1212) out of the Chinese Pure Land teachings. Salvation is by calling on the name Amida in prayer. His pupil, Shinran (1173–1262), followed in his footsteps but took the Pure Land teachings a stage further. He believed that adherence to the Vinaya was an attachment of pride, and, as such, a negative attribute. He recognized no difference between monk and layman, decided that celibacy was not a requirement and married, and did much to advance the cause of women. His teachings now constitute the largest sect in Japan, the Jodoshinsu, the True Pure Land sect.

Nichiren (1222–82) espoused a zealous intolerance with his reformed Tendai sect. He attempted to blend religious and nationalistic elements, insisting that his was the only true religion and that all others should be suppressed, and preferably suppressed with violence. In his eyes, the Lotus Sutra contained the most powerful truth and he himself was an incarnation of Shaka, one of the four Japanese Buddhas. Exiled twice, he nevertheless gathered a sound following which still exists today.

ZEN BUDDHISM

The great path has no gates,
Thousands of roads enter it
When one passes through this gateless gate
He walks freely between heaven and earth.

Ekai, called Mumon (1183–1260 CE), The Gateless Gate

Possibly the most famous of the Japanese Buddhist schools in Western eyes is Zen Buddhism (in Chinese – Ch'an). It took root in Japan c.1200 with Eisai (1141–1215) who brought back the Rinzai school, and his pupil, Dogen (1200–53), who introduced the Soto school. Zen in general, and Rinzai Zen in particular, appealed to the samurai class, and the aristocracy, who liked its simplicity, austerity, devotion, generosity of spirit – and its humour. Eisai taught that satori (sudden enlightenment) is attained through the medium of strict meditation, the paradox of koans (impossible questions), ceremonial rites such as tea-drinking, and art – ikebana (flower-arranging), painting and calligraphy and poetry, particularly the haiku form. Soto Zen appealed to the farmer, fisherman and peasant class, because it stressed discipline, work, practice and philosophical questions as the way to realize one's Buddha-nature.

Zen is Buddhist mysticism. It is the only path which uses strict method in its preparation for the mystical. Meditation is not just a tool of itself, it requires the absolution of the technique to underpin the devotion. The technique is almost as important as the act of meditating itself. This ritual removes any unpredictable elements. Anyone who follows the prescribed instruction may venture onto this Way, and effectively the immersion of self onto the Way must be regarded as part of the arriving.

Buddhist meditation is one of the means towards liberation from suffering, and when the meditator embarks on his quest there are fixed precepts laid down on which to meditate.

A student of Tendai, a philosophical school of Buddhism, came to the Zen abode of Gasan as a pupil. When he was departing a few years later, Gasan warned him: 'Studying the truth speculatively is useful as a way of collecting preaching material. But remember that unless you meditate constantly your light of truth may go out.'

In Zen, it is flexible – as in emptying your mind and letting what will enter, without thinking about it, without commenting on it, without censoring it – just experiencing it. This is the 'nothing' of Zen. Start from the premise of nothing and see what you gain.

Zen is about being, as in this Zen tale, 'Inch Time Foot Gem'.

A lord asked Takuan, a Zen teacher, to suggest how he might pass the time. He felt his days very long attending his office and sitting stiffly to receive the homage of others. Takuan wrote eight Chinese characters and gave them to the man:
Not twice this day
Inch time foot gem.
This day will not come again.
Each minute is worth a priceless gem.

In everything, the experience is at one with the person experiencing it – be it, let it be you – there is no divide. Umon (d.949) said:

When walking, just walk,
When sitting just sit,
Above all, don't wobble.

In Zen, being in the centre of being is important. But man moves from the centre. He looks for an abundance of self, for whatever it is that he feels defines him, most obviously in the accumulation of material goods as the definition of happiness. He loses contact with his centre, his point of humanness. Zen is not about giving up part of the self, it is a question of coming back to the centre, where everything is transcendent – yet very ordinary. One Zen master's advice to his pupils was that they should, 'Carry on an ordinary task, without attachments. Shit and piss, wear your clothes, eat your meals. When you're tired, lie down. The fool will laugh at you, but the wise man will understand.' Be true to the centre.

To start on the path, there must be the will to start. Openness (no preconceptions) is required:

> Nan-in, a Japanese master during the Meiji era (1868–1912), received a university professor who came to enquire about Zen. Nan-in served tea. He poured his visitor's cup full, and then kept on pouring.
>
> The professor watched the overflow until he could no longer restrain himself. 'It is overfull. No more will go in!'
>
> 'Like this cup,' Nan-in said, 'you are full of your own opinions and speculations. How can I show you Zen unless you first empty your cup?'

Anyone who starts on the path to Zen must be prepared for unquestioning obedience to his master. But it is obedience with thought, merely a tool to subjugate the dominating ego and to cultivate the mindfulness required in every aspect of life. This frees the mind just when it is least expected.

> When Banzan was walking through a market he overheard a conversation between a butcher and his customer.
>
> 'Give me the best piece of meat you have,' said the customer.
>
> 'Everything in my shop is the best,' replied the butcher. 'You cannot find here any piece of meat that is not the best.'
>
> At these words Banzan became enlightened.

One of the most illuminating methods of Zen teaching is wrestling with koans – abstruse questions (or riddles) which have no answer that can be divined by normal methods. The master asks the student, 'In clapping both hands a sound is heard: what is the sound of one hand?' It is one of the first of the koans that is asked. The other is, 'A monk asked Master Joshu, "Does a dog have Buddha-nature?" Master Joshu answered 'Mu!'" [Mu, the Chinese negative symbol, means 'nay', 'no-thing', 'non-existence'.] The pupil puts all of himself into solving this problem, until the solution arrives and he is at one with the koan. Only then will he realize the difference between explanation and understanding.

Understanding, or seeing, is involvement; explanation or observing is detachment. And yet both detachment and

161

involvement are the ultimate, in which identification (not only with self and with others, but with everything) is total.

> After Bankei had passed away, a blind man who lived near the master's temple told a friend: 'Since I am blind, I cannot watch a person's face, so I must judge his character by the sound of his voice. Ordinarily when I hear someone congratulate another upon his happiness or success, I also hear a secret tone of envy. When condolence is expressed for the misfortune of another, I hear pleasure and satisfaction, as if the one condoling was really glad there was something left to gain in his own world.
>
> In all my experience, however, Bankei's voice was always sincere. Whenever he expressed happiness, I heard nothing but happiness, and whenever he express sorrow, sorrow was all I heard.

Concentration, meditation, koans, letting go, involvement, mindfulness: these lead to satori, the blinding flash of enlightenment.

> A Zen master named Gisan asked a young student to bring him a pail of water to cool his bath. The student brought the water and, after cooling the bath, threw onto the ground the little that was left over.
>
> 'You dunce!' the master scolded him. 'Why didn't you give the rest of the water to the plants? What right have you to waste even a drop of water in this temple?'
>
> The young student attained Zen in that instant. He changed his name to Tekisui, which means a drop of water.

In an instant the connectedness of everything may be understood. But it is inexplicable and has no description – that too is part of satori. Perhaps one who has achieved enlightenment should try to explain, if only to encourage others to take the same or similar path. But the explanation of the experience must never be taken for the real thing: the finger pointing at the moon is not the moon. Experience is the only way.

> An instant realization sees endless time.
> Endless time is as one moment.
> When one comprehends the endless moment
> He realizes the person who is seeing it.
>
> The Gateless Gate

4 • ORIGINS
PRIMAL RELIGIONS

The popular Western perception of primal religions – the so-called primitive religions – is that they are animistic, ancestor-worshipping, sacrificial, fetishistic, ritualistic, shamanistic, superstitious and, at best, polytheistic. The truth is rather different. But there are now many local and indigenous interpreters and scholars who are taking a greater interest in their spiritual heritage whose fruitful findings are contributing to a greater understanding of these faiths.

Most tribal and primal societies have a very strong social structure, around which much religion is based. Each serves to reinforce the other – often one without the other would be meaningless. In all of them dignity – in life and in death – is paramount. Everything has its reasons, and everything has its place. There is also a surprising tolerance. Most groups recognize that their beliefs are theirs, and do not necessarily cater for the community next door. So of course there are differences, a veritable plurality of beliefs, myths, cosmologies and rituals.

Although they vary considerably around the world, the primal religions are all concerned, to a greater or lesser degree, with about half a dozen or so seminal beliefs. And contrary to most people's understandings, most primal religions are monotheistic. They all give credence to the power of the spirits – mostly because they are obliged to live close to the natural world and are dependent on it for survival. Most of them practise some sort of ancestor veneration, partly because death is often closer to these societies than to ours and becoming an ancestor is a way of either 'cheating' death, or some version of an afterlife. Most involve some elements of prayer, offering or sacrifice, and most involve a medicine man or shaman or witchdoctor – but not necessarily in the pejorative terms in which it is understood in the 'civilized' world. Finally, most of them have some kind of New Season, or New Year celebrations, closely connected with the eternal round of nature and deeply life-affirming.

What follows is an outline, not of all primal religions, but of the reasonably widespread and general attributes of religions in Africa, Australia, New Zealand, Melanesia and North America. There are themes common to all, but what comes across most strongly is the communication and interaction with both the perceived and unperceived world around them. It is striking how close most of these people are to their god or gods and to the forces that drive them, the energies of life, and the now-ness of things.

AFRICA

With probably as many religions as tribal groupings, African religious beliefs and practices vary in complexity across the continent. Where the tribal grouping is nomadic and pastoral, dependent on finding food, life is simple and religious emphasis is on the relationship with nature. Much of the life of nomadic cultures centres on the cow, which is semi-sacred because vital to life. If the tribal group is fixed in some more abundant area, such as close to the lakes of Central Africa, there is cultivation and time to subscribe to a richer cosmogony – not only of the connection with nature, but also with divinities.

Indigenous religions generally subscribe to a hierarchy. At the base are rocks, earth, grass. Then animals, with man supreme among them. Next are the more powerful spiritual men, and ancestors, then the divinities and the quite remote Supreme God. Most believe in a Creator God, who, having created, is too great, powerful and distant to be worshipped directly. Just occasionally he is called on in an emergency; he is presumed, however, to see over all. The Ila describe him as, 'He has no when, no where, he comes to no end.' He is regarded as benevolent, but unpredictable. Man talks to lesser beings, to nature and other intermediaries because he cannot get close to God.

Most religious activity revolves around lesser gods, spirits which inhabit all things, and, particularly, ancestors. All are the interceders between man, his environment and God, but ancestors are particularly revered. They, after all, have intimate knowledge of the living, and now have superior knowledge and other, perhaps mystical, powers which they can use to help the living. At the very least they are venerated and sometimes even worshipped as gods. But their role is mainly as mediators and facilitators. They watch over their community and warn against the breaking of taboos.

At the same time, even though ancestors occupy a special place, death is not welcomed. It is always regarded as unnatural, except in extreme old age. It is a paradox – feared, and yet dying provides the gateway to becoming an ancestor. Because there is no doctrine of reincarnation, except with the Ashanti, ancestral spirits live on in the world, sometimes inhabiting the living, sometimes not, but ever-present.

There is an understanding of the underlying relationship between man, community, animal, plant and the god or gods. All care is taken not to break this net. Many rites are directed towards its maintenance, or to its reparation, if broken. Religion in Africa means being in the world. It is the understanding of the place of everything as much as the shared tradition which binds the community.

Most tribal groups have ceremonies for all the rites of passage: birth, naming, initiation, marriage and death. Rites affirm the solidarity of the community and recognize man's responsibility for nature and dependence on the wider spirit world. Initiation takes various forms, mostly as an induction into adulthood, occasionally as entry into secret societies. These societies are sometimes the only means of gaining access to a particular livelihood such as healing. Marriage is vital to all communities in Africa, as are children. Being unmarried, or being barren is a sign that the 'net' of relationships is damaged or broken, and some reparation is required.

Almost all African cultures use sacrifice of some sort. It takes many forms. In the nomadic tribal groupings it is often the cow, the most important currency, which is sacrificed to the one God. In the 'technologically' more advanced, richer, groups it is the giving of gifts – not necessarily to the supreme deity, but to ancestors in acknowledgement of their powers. A great deal of ritual is given over to ancestral or funeral rites. The breaking of taboos, or even worse, actions against the community, necessitate sacrifice and collective expiation. There is a great understanding of total involvement on all levels – mundane and spiritual.

Spirit-possession, either for healing or divination, is used throughout Africa. The medium occupies a special place in the community and is called on for many things – healing, divination, exorcism. But spirit-possession may also be involuntary and (possibly) evil and affect the ordinary man rather than the expert, in which case the medium, the nganga, will find the cause and solution. The medium, with his abilities to interpret and to heal, represents the closeness of man to the spirit world.

Islam and Christianity have both made enormous inroads into the tribal practices of Africa. The country's religions have always been open to a reinterpreting of traditions as circumstances change (this is not to say that the old traditions have fallen by the wayside, merely that they move with the times), and these two universal religions have been both absorbed into the traditions and also have imbibed a certain amount of local practice in order to become acceptable. There are quite a number of charismatic and evangelical and millennial movements throughout the country, which use eclectic elements from all sources. But tradition lives on regardless. Its primacy is too deep, too concerned with the day-to-day living in the world, to be fully eradicated.

OCEANIA

Oceania covers a large part of the globe, from Irian Jaya in the West to Easter Island in the East, from Hawaii in the North to New Zealand in the South. This area includes Australasia, Melanesia, Polynesia, Micronesia. It is the geography that ties them together because even though there is a certain homogeneity in Oceania, each island has its own special emphasis. There are enough similarities between the various areas to make some limited assumptions, but what follows is a flavour of the diversity that may be found among these extraordinary peoples.

AUSTRALIA

The Aborigines were thought to have no religion by early Christian missionaries because they found no outward signs and symbols as they understood them. Rather, the Aborigines do not separate life from the sacred. Unless you adhere to certain principles, life simply does not work. There is a deep affinity with the natural world; co-existence is vital.

Native Australians believe that the spirit in self, in rock, water, tree, animal is one and the same and is mutually interdependent. Also, that particular animals or plants have an identification and a special relationship with a tribal group and act as guardians. Each tribal group has descended from some particular mythic ancestor which is taken as the group's totem. Those descended from the kangaroo, for instance, have the responsibility both to care for the animal and to ensure plentiful supplies of kangaroo meat for the community. It reinforces the links between all lives.

The world is deemed to have been created. Although a Sky God is supposed, he plays no part in the lives of men. It is the totemic ancestors who once walked the earth in a period known as the 'Dreamtime' who are venerated. All myths and stories centre around these ancestors and this time when everything was perfect. All practices and rituals are concerned with the continuation of the moral precepts laid down by those ancestors in the 'Dreamtime'. And morality is conformation to traditions.

Death is just a transition from one kind of life to another. The spirit does not go to another place, it stays around, part of the community, a spiritual existence side by side with the natural. It is another link between man and the world around him, providing not so much continuity, more a circularity.

Elders and medicine men are the knowledgeable ones. They are all male. There are initiation rites involving circumcision and the spilling of blood – or, if not blood, then red ochre.

Women's ceremonies are also secret, mostly to do with fertility. But it is men who enact the myths (that are both contained within the rites and explain the rites) through storytelling, song, dance, painting. It is men who guard the storyboards, on which the myths are scratched in patterns, known as bull-roarers. They also have ceremonies for the increase of the food supply – being nomadic there is no direct control. Special rites, involving songs and dances, and the letting of blood, or the spilling of red ochre are used to ensure a plentiful supply of food.

It has not been easy for the Australian Aborigine. Christianity came into their ordered world and made no sense, being unconcerned with the eternal relationship between man, nature and his ancestors. There has been a decimation of the old traditions over the last two centuries, but there are signs of a revival. The Aborigine is nothing if not spiritual – materialism barely impinges – but it could be hard to maintain old ways in the face of encroaching 'civilization'.

NEW ZEALAND

The Maoris share some features of the Polynesian religions, such as myths of Mother Earth and Father Sky Creator Gods, who were eventually separated by their sons. The sons became immortals who created the earth and the human race. The life force is the essence of everything and is a gift from the gods.

Maoris have a three-tier universe, the sky, the world of light and the world of the dead. Io is the supreme God and the source of all power but is known to only a few initiates. The land is sacred, as is the universe. Having your land is vital, you are nothing without it. Consequently care must be taken in order to hold it in trust for future generations.

There are no temples in Maori culture, but certain places were dedicated by a priest to the veneration of a particular god. Sacrifice was not usual, except occasionally of food in order to placate a god. Only in time of war was ritual killing used. The first enemy killed was dedicated to the god of war and it was considered necessary to eat the heart of your defeated opponent – this conferred his strength to you. (This theme of cannibalism, the transfer of power by eating your enemies, is found frequently in some of the primal religions.) Or, when a new meeting house was built, the body of a slave was buried beneath the main pole. At gatherings, such as for funeral rites, the open space in front of this building was regarded as sacred.

The most important rites in the Maori canon are those of birth and, particularly, death. At birth there is a ritual prayer to confer spiritual power on the child and a feast of welcome. There is no initiation because the fact of birth confers membership of the community. Death rituals are long and elaborate, designed both to placate the spirit of the departed and to speed him on his way and to return the family to normal life after being involved with the tapu of death. Tapus are necessary for the preserving of morality, they are prohibitions, the breaking of which have dangerous effects and can only be neutralized by purification in running water.

Some Maori culture has been retained and one may catch glimpses of what it was. But it seems to exist today within the context of a predominantly Christian society. But there is pride in the understanding of the land and its spirits and the values embodied in the respect of ancestors.

Melanesia (includes Fiji, Solomon Islands, New Caledonia, Vanuatu)

For some cultures it is hard to separate the sacred from the secular. Rites are practised as everyday life, before hunting, planting, marriage. Religion, as we know it, is bound up in the totality of life. It is recognized as the enduring relationship and communion between man and nature, man and spirit, man and environment, etc. Some have a concept of 'in the Beginning' from which all have fallen, and many ceremonies and beliefs (except that they are not beliefs as such, they simply are) are the eternal attempt to get back to that beginning when all was perfect.

Throughout Melanesia the permanent relationship between the living and their ancestor-spirits is by far the most important element. Ancestor-spirits have access to supernatural powers and have the ability to maintain the life and prosperity of the living or to cause them trouble. These spirits are closer to the earth and to the living than gods. Indeed, there is little curiosity about the origins of the world, although it is assumed that some gods created the world and provided man with the means to live. But because it is this world that is important, there is more communication between man and his ancestors than with the gods. Most rites are directed at keeping these links forged.

Rituals vary from those that deal with everyday life, hunting, fishing, etc, to those of birth, initiation and funerals. There is much feasting and dancing and telling of stories. Sorcerers abound – sympathetic magic, healing, divination, protection from evil – and the sorcerer holds an important part in the society. He is often (dis)credited with deaths, since most deaths are deemed to be the fault of someone. There are elaborate initiation rites for young men. Through all these, the ancestors are called on for their help.

The Melanesian identity is well-rooted in its ancient traditions and, except during the first incursions of foreign religions, its religion remains alive and vital to this day. It has managed to syncretize what it needs and local Christianity has adapted to the requirements of the Melanesians. But it did cause quite some difficulty when the universal religions first arrived. In Melanesia, power is supposed, essentially, to be a question of religion, and many took to European ways, including Christianity, assuming European prosperity would follow as a matter of course. It certainly demonstrates the unbridgeable gulf between a culture whose whole ethos was one of sharing and one whose ethos rested mostly in individual power through commerce. Disappointments ensued, giving rise to many new religious movements. These movements were often dedicated to the renewal of myth and practice, were deeply atavistic, and yet, as such, are responsible for today's vigour. But in some places it gave rise to the Cargo Cults.

Cargo Cults

These are often regarded as ridiculous by the world outside, but there is an ethos which lies behind them. Melanesians find it difficult to understand that certain people or groups are not willing to share goods and power with those that do not have those commodities. In order to accrue some of what they lack to themselves, they turn to the traditional myths, in which there are five principal themes: that a messiah will return; that the world will end soon; that mankind is divided into two groups as a result of the actions of two brothers; that these two brothers, separated through hostility, will be reconciled; that eventually all peoples, divided through misfortune, should one day be united in shared prosperity.

Very often it is through the medium of a prophet who foresees the coming of a messiah perhaps, or the return of ancestor-spirits with supplies of manufactured goods brought by planes or ships. The cult of the cargo: when all

Melanesians will receive all they want and deserve, but when primarily all suffering and difficulty will end, harmony and honour will return and the proper way of life will be restored. Sometimes the normal daily routine is totally disrupted in preparation for the arrival of this fabled cargo (for cargo also read salvation) and its attendant new life. When it doesn't, reasons are found, but it does not detract from the myth itself, which lives on and surfaces again and again in a similar movement somewhere else.

NORTH AMERICA

We consider Judaism ancient at about 4,000 years old. But it is said that the origins of some of the primal religions of North America are at least ten times as old. A beautiful thought but meaningless, because for most of us the first century CE is hard enough to understand. To conceive of practices that are 30,000 to 40,000 years old is like an average person's understanding of the theory of relativity – or even why a light bulb works.

Not only are the roots of the North American Indian old, but there is a great plurality and diversity of tradition, language, physical type, geographical area and climate. But there are themes which are more or less universal. Although there are several creation myths, many tribes and peoples believed in one great Creator Spirit, along with the Earth Mother.

'The Great Spirit is our father, but the earth is our mother. She nourishes us; that which we put into the ground she returns to us, and healing plants she gives us likewise. If we are wounded, we go to our mother and seek to lay the wounded part against her, to be healed.'
Bedagi of the Wabanakis Nation, 1900

'We saw the Great Spirit's work in everything: sun, moon, trees, wind and mountains. Sometimes we approached him through these things ... I think we have a true belief in the supreme being ...'
Tatanga Mani, Stoney Indian, 1871–1967

Nature's powers and the ideal of the sacred have a mutual dependency (a metaphysics of nature). 'Holy Mother Earth, the trees and all nature, are witnesses of your thoughts and deeds' (a Winnebago wise saying). Sacred areas and sacred symbols such as stones or trees, are not for worship, they are for understanding the thread that runs between the occult and the manifest, the link between the sacred and the secular.

Everything as it moves, now and then, here and there, makes stops. The bird as it flies stops in one place to make its nest, and in another to rest in its flight. A man when he goes forth stops when he wills. So the god has stopped. The sun, which is so bright and beautiful, is one place where he has stopped. The moon, the stars, the winds, he has been with. The trees, the animals, are all where he has stopped, and the Indian thinks of these places and sends his prayers there to reach the place where the god has stopped and win help and a blessing.

Old Dakota wiseman, 1890

The North American Indian had a comprehension of nature and the earth and of his place within it; he had a responsibility to care for it and knew that all life is sacred, not just at times of worship.

What is life? It is the flash of a firefly in the night. It is the breath of a buffalo in the wintertime. It is the little shadow which runs across the grass and loses itself in the Sunset.

Crowfoot, of the Blackfoot Indians, 1821–90

He was concerned (as with most primal religions) with living here and now, with the continuity of existence and the cycles of seasons.

I wonder if the ground has anything to say? ... I hear what the ground says. The ground says, It is the great Spirit that placed me here. The great Spirit tells me to take care of the Indians, to feed them aright. The Great Spirit, in placing men on the earth, desired then to take good care of the ground and to do each other no harm ...

Cayuse Chief, 1855

Because most tribes were nomadic and depended on hunting, the relationship between man and animal was very particular. Hunting success often depended on a good relationship with the spirit that owned each animal, and rites were conducted to ensure that the spirit was favourable. These spirits were hierarchical, reflecting the hierarchy of the tribe, and were bound under one great ruling spirit. Sometimes the owner of an animal was the same spirit as a tribal guardian. The interrelation between the worlds of mass and spirit, of animal and vegetable, is sacred and must be preserved at all times.

> Kinship with all creatures of the earth, sky and water was a real and active principle. For the animal and bird world there existed a brotherly feeling that kept the Lakota safe among them and so close to their feathered and furred friends that in true brotherhood they spoke a common tongue.
>
> Chief Luther Standing Bear of the Lakota, b.1868

The Great Spirit is at the centre of a circle and the concept of the circle was vital in every area of life. It was seen not only in the sun, moon and stars, but in the never-ending round of the seasons, in worship, in art, in living. It was also referred to as the 'sacred hoop of the nation'. While the circle was whole, all was well.

> Everything an Indian does is in a circle, and that is because the Power of the World always works in circles, and everything tries to be round. The Sky is round and I have heard the earth is round like a ball and so are all the stars. The Wind, in its greatest power, whirls. Birds make their nests in circles, for theirs is the same religion as ours. The sun comes forth and goes down again in a circle. The moon does the same, and both are round.
>
> Even the seasons form a great circle in their changing, and always come back again to where they were. The life of a man is a circle from childhood to childhood and so it is in everything where power moves.
>
> Black Elk, of the Oglala Teton Dakota, 1931

Man was enjoined to work towards perfection, and perfection was generally sought in this life, through the understanding of natural and sacred patterns. The idea was to become indivisible, both personally and communally, from the worlds around. Man is also at the centre of the circle, but in the centre of a circle that is divided into four equal parts, the symbol of wholeness, each part mutually interdependent. Four, among many tribes, particularly the Sioux, is a sacred number: it stands for the four quarters of the earth, the four seasons, elements, divisions of time (day, night, moon, year), the four stages of life (babyhood, childhood, adulthood, old age) — everything. It expresses a total harmony and unity;

the concept of partnership between man, life, nature and spirit.

Today, the Navajo Indian understands that man is a whole: that everything is interrelated within and without. He is macrocosm and microcosm, contains the seeds of all things within him and represents all things. Everything in the universe should be balanced and harmonious – and it is a very fine balance, easy to knock askew. It requires great dedication and understanding to keep true.

Much of the American Indian has been wiped away by the influx of white people, with all their attendant drives, desires and beliefs. There are syncretic Christian/Indian movements today which bear little relation to original tribal lore. But it is necessary to live in the world as it is – and although much is lost, many Indian peoples are finding truth and solace in the traditions of their Elders, achieving a harmony that is often difficult to find in any part of the world today.

EPILOGUE

Some of these primal religions show just how far we have deviated from the care and reverence for the world around us. We could learn a great deal from them about how we might better live in harmony with the natural world. We could also benefit from the radiance that comes from interaction with the spirit that resides in all things. It could be construed as an earthy form of the Tao.

> Before talking of holy things, we prepare ourselves by offerings ... one will fill his pipe and hand it to the other who will light it and offer it to the sky and earth ... they will smoke together ... Then they will be ready to talk.
> Chased-by-Bears, a Santee-Yanktonai Sioux

GLOSSARY

Ark   cupboard in the Jerusalem facing wall of a synagogue which contains the scrolls of the Torah. (Also, originally, a small portable temple)

Ashkenazi   one of the two main cultural groups of Judaism, the other being Sephardi, based principally in northern and eastern Europe

Bar Mitzvah   ceremony during which Jewish boys, at thirteen, become adults

Bat Mitzvah   ceremony during which Jewish girls, at twelve, become adults

Covenant   a bargain or agreement in Judaism between God and man

Diaspora   the scattering of any community or nation, but in particular the spread of the Jews around the world, away from their intrinsic roots

En Sof   name used in the Kabbalah for God

Haggadah   moral teaching from midrashic expositions of Hebrew texts

Halakhah   legal teaching based on midrashic expositions

Hanukkah (Dedication)   eight-day Jewish festival marking the rededication of the temple in Jerusalem in 164 BCE

176

Hasidism mystical movement, founded in eighteenth century by Baal Shem Tov, with Kabbalistic roots

Holocaust the name given to Hitler's 'final solution' – the extermination of six million Jews in gas ovens during the Second World War

Jacob one of the three principal patriarchs

Kabbalah mystical tradition of which the most famous book is the Zohar, Book of Splendours, a Midrash on the Pentateuch

Messiah (anointed one) the person chosen by God to be king

Midrash method of exposition of the Hebrew texts designed to reveal the inner meaning the Torah

Mishnah a compilation of oral teachings which formed the basis of the Talmud

Moses Father of Judaism, received the Torah from God on Mount Sinai

Passover (Pesach) the seven-day festival commemorating the deliverance of the Jews from Egypt

Patriarch father-figure, especially founding fathers, i.e. Abraham, Isaac, Jacob

Pentateuch the first five books of the Bible (Genesis, Exodus, Leviticus, Numbers, Deuteronomy)

Pentecost harvest festival, 52 days after Passover

Pharisee anti–nationalist party which emerged in the second century BCE. Kept the faith alive after the fall of Jerusalem in 70 CE through religious rather than political means (see Saducees)

Phylacteries (Tephillin) small boxes, worn on arms and head, containing scriptural texts

Progressive covers both Liberal and Reform movements, highly critical of Talmudic fundamentalism and orthodoxy in many things

The Prophets the second division of the Hebrew Bible

Rabbi 'master', religious teacher and interpreter of the Torah. Today, a preacher, leader of synagogue worship, minister to the community

Rosh Hashana the New Year, looking forward to the Messiah and the Kingdom of God

Saducees nationalist party, aristocratic collaborators with Rome, rose also in the second century BCE with the Pharisees, also determined to keep Judaism alive in a political way

Shabbat (Sabbath) day of worship and rest from Friday sunset to Saturday sunset. It is the seventh day of creation. Reminds the faithful of the deliverance from Egypt

Shavuot (Pentecost) feast seven weeks after Passover

Shema the confession of faith: 'Hear O Israel, the Lord our God, the Lord is one'

Synagogue meeting place for worship and study

Tabernacle Sukkot, week-long festival at the end of harvest

Talmud the written interpretation of the Hebrew scriptures

Torah (i) the five books of the Law, the Pentateuch, the first division of the Hebrew Bible, (ii) God's teachings to Israel (iii) the order both of the universe and of moral and spiritual instruction

Yhwh (Yahweh, Jehovah) the sacred unspeakable name of God, means 'I am'

Yom Kippur Day of Atonement, day of fasting and repentance, most solemn day of the year

Zionism movement to establish a permanent Jewish state

CHRISTIANITY

Apostle one of the twelve original followers of Jesus Christ

Baptism the sacrament of entry through the medium of water into the Christian Church

Bishop most senior order of ministry in (most of) the Christian Church with authority to ordain priests

Confirmation acceptance into the Church by laying on of hands on those already baptized. Orthodox churches perform it at baptism, Roman Catholics at age seven, others at puberty

Coptic Church Church of Egypt, monophysite (i.e. rejects teachings about the incarnation of Christ)

Counter-Reformation revival and reform of the RC church due to the inroads of the Reformation

Covenant bargain or agreement marked by the death of Jesus

Easter movable (dependent on the moon) festival commemorating the resurrection of Christ

Eucharist the sharing of the bread and wine at communion, commemorating the Last Supper of Christ

Holy Spirit the third person in the Trinity

Lent forty-day period of penitence and fasting before Easter

Liturgy the words of the services of the Christian Church

Luther, Martin 1483–1546, founder of the German Reformation. Faith in Jesus Christ is the only justification, therefore hierarchy is unnecessary

Patriarch the head of one of the Eastern Orthodox churches

Paul, St Saul, a former Pharisee, instrumental in the spread of Christianity throughout the then known world

Pentecost marks the coming of the Holy Spirit on the Apostles, also the start of the Church; second most important Christian festival for the Church

Pope head of the Roman Catholic Church, also known Bishop of Rome, Vicar of Christ. Infallible in his pronouncements

Reformation the movement, in the Christian Churches, between the fourteenth and seventeenth centuries, which led to the separate formation of the Protestant church. The authority of the Pope was denied, some doctrinal issues and accessibility to the scriptures were the main differences

Russian Orthodox Church almost unchanged in certain aspects since the tenth century CE. Although driven underground by Communism, now coming to the fore

Sacrament 'The outward and visible sign of an inward and spiritual grace' (Book of Common Prayer). Protestant (Reformed) Churches count baptism and the Eucharist as the only two sacraments, whereas the Roman Catholic and Orthodox Churches also consider confirmation, marriage, ordination, penance and extreme unction – or anointing of the sick – as sacraments

Trinity God as three persons, all equal and one – the Father, Son and Holy Spirit

Islam

Abu Bakr   Muhammad's father-in-law

Ali   fourth caliph, cousin and son-in-law of Muhammad

Al-juma   assembly for prayer

Allah   the Supreme God. Allah is one: there are no other gods

Black Stone   sacred stone set into the Ka'bah in Mecca, said to have been received by Ishmael from Gabriel

Caliph   title of the leaders of the Muslim community after the death of Muhammad

Creed   La ilaha illa Allah, 'There is no other God but God and Muhammad is his prophet'

Fatwa   a sentence of death

Five Pillars of Islam   shahada; salat; zakat; sawm; hajj (*see* p.37)

Hadith   traditions, teachings and sayings of Muhammad which are not found in the Qur'an but which are recognized as authoritative

Hajj   pilgrimage to Mecca, one of the Five Pillars

Hijra   going forth, the migration of Muhammad from Mecca to Medina; seminal because Medina became the centre of Islam. Muslims count calendar years 'after hijra'

'Id Al-Adha   the great festival of the Islamic year, coinciding with the sacrifice at Mina

'Id Al-Fitr   the end of the fast of Ramadan

Ijma   consensus of opinion in the Muslim community

Imam   (i) Sunni religious leader and teacher (ii) in Shi'a Islam, every age produces an imam who makes contemporary the teachings of Muhammad

Ismailis   a Shi'a sect who believe that the seventh imam was the final one who disappeared and will return on the last day

Jihad   literally striving; the promulgation of Islam by force, or the battle within oneself to become a true Muslim

Ka'bah   the sanctuary in Mecca toward which all Muslims pray

Mecca   holy city of Islam, the centre for pilgrimage

Mosque   place of public worship

Muezzin he who calls the faithful to prayer in the mosque
Qur'an the Word of God, the Islamic holy book, the revelation to Muhammad
Quraysh the tribe from which Muhammad came
Ramadan the 30 days of fasting in the ninth month of the Muslim year
Salat ritual prayer, carried out five times a day facing Mecca
Sawm fasting, particularly in the month of Ramadan
Shahada recitation of the creed, the fundamental belief of a Muslim
Shari'a the body of law for Muslims which derives from the Qur'an and the Sunna and is authoritative
Shi'a the minority, 10 per cent, group of Muslims
Sufism mystical, ascetic movement, founded in the eighth century CE
Sunnah 'Trodden Path', the most important authority after the Qur'an in lawmaking – refers to the words and actions of Muhammad and, less so, to the first four caliphs
Sunni the majority, 90 per cent of Muslims
Ulama the interpreters of the Shari'a, upholders of orthodoxy
Umma the Muslim community
Zakat alms-giving, obligatory, one of the five pillars of Islam

ZOROASTRIANISM

Ahura Mazda/Ohrmazd Wise Lord, the Zoroastrian God, the force of total Good
Amesha Spentas Bounteous Immortals, representing aspects of Ahura Mazda with earthly correspondences: see Spenta Mainyu and Asha, Vohu Mana, Armaiti, Kshathara, Haurvatat, Ameretat. Later, angels in the fight against evil
Angra Mainyu/Ahriman the Evil Spirit in constant battle with Ahura Mazda
Ameretat Immortality. Plants
Armaiti Devotion. Earth
Aryans literally, 'noble ones', Indo-Iranians *c.* 2000 BCE

Asha   Truth, Righteousness. Fire
Avesta   the scriptures
Chinvat Bridge   bridge over which the dead pass into the next life: the good cross easily, the bad fall off into torment
Daevas   demons
Druj   lie
Frashokereti   the renovation of creation
Gathas   hymns in the central part of the Yasna
Gayomart   first man
Haurvatat   Wholeness. Water
Kshathara   Dominion. Sky
Kusti   sacred thread of initiation
Magi   priestly class of ancient Persia
Spenta Mainyu (Holy Spirit)   the force for good, the possible twin of Angra Mainyu
Yashts   hymns
Yasna   the liturgical part of the Avesta

HINDUISM

Advaita   non-dualism, 'Advaita Vedanta is the philosophy which teaches that ultimate reality lies beyond the individual condition outside the dualism of subject and object in which thought operates' (Elements of Hinduism).
Agni   God of Fire
Ahimsa   non-violence, not harming, respect for life
Aryan   name given to the peoples who invaded India c.2000 BCE
Ashrama   stage of life
Atman   soul, spirit, self
Avatar   incarnation, literally one who descends
Bhagavad Gita   'Song of the Lord', scriptures, from the Mahabharata, 4–2 BCE
Bhakti   devotion to God
Bhakti yoga   path of love leading to moksha
Brahma   Hindu Lord of Creation, one of the Trimurti
Brahman   God, the Ultimate Reality, the Supreme Spirit
Brahmin   the priestly class, a priest

Dharma   duty, universal, the righteous duty of things, the proper way to act, the social order, the way things should be

Divali, Diwali   festival of lights, marks the return of Rama from exile and his reunion with Sita

Durga   goddess, 'the inacessible', consort of Shiva

Ganesha   the elephant-headed god, son of Shiva, god of good beginnings

Garuda   the devourer, Vishnu's mount

Gunas   the three strands or qualities in which all matter is composed in various proportions, interwoven like the strands of a rope: sattva, rajas and tamas

Guru   spiritual teacher

Hanuman   monkey god in the Ramayana

Holi   Spring festival which celebrates the love of Krishna for Rahda, often with boisterous games

Jati   caste

Jiva   the self of matter that experiences the cycle of samsara

Jnana yoga   path of knowledge to moksha

Kali   the black goddess

Kali Yuga   the last of the four ages, and the worst

Kalpa   an aeon, a day of Brahma, 1000 ages, a period of 4320 million years as mortals count them

Kama   desire, Eros

Karma   law of cause and effect, action and reaction

Krishna   incarnation, avatar of Vishnu, found in the Bhagavad Gita

Kshatriya   the warrior, princely class

Laxmi   Goddess of light and wealth, wife of Vishnu

Mahabharata   a smriti scripture, 9 BCE

Mantra   a repeated chant or prayer

Maya   illusion, power of creation

Moksha   release from samsara, liberation from the ties of life

Parshad   food offered at a shrine

Parvati   wife of Shiva

Puja   devotional offering

Puranas   devotional texts

Rajas   second of the gunas: dust, passion or activity

Sama   avatar of Vishnu, in the Ramayana

Samsara   eternal cycle of birth and death and rebirth

Sanatama dharma   the eternal faith, the eternal dharma

Sannyasin   last stage of life, also a spiritual seeker and a renouncer of the world

Sarasvati   consort of Brahma, goddess of truth

Sattva   first of the gunas, goodness or light

Shakti   female aspect of God, cosmic energy

Shiva   One of the Trimurti – destruction

Shudra   servant class

Smriti   remembered scriptures

Shruti   revealed scriptures, Vedas, Upanishads

Tamas   the third of the gunas: darkness, inertia or heaviness

Trimurti   the trinity of Brahman, Vishnu and Shiva – the three main aspects of God

Untouchables   class with no caste and excluded from normal social life

Upanishads   the last books of the Vedas, the Vedanta

Vaishya   the merchant class

Varna   class, see Brahmin, Kshatriya, Vaishya, Shudra

Varnashrama dharma   the duties or right way of living appropriate for each class and stage of life

Vedas   Shruti scripture, 1500 BCE, most sacred text, comprising the Rig-Veda, the Sama-Veda, the Yajur-Veda and the Atharva-Veda

Vishnu   one of the Trimurti, the preserver, appears as Rama and Krishna

BUDDHISM

Abhidharma-pitaka   basket of higher teachings, part of the Tipitaka

Aimsa   doctrine of non-violence

Amitabha or Amida Buddha   buddha of infinite light, pure land

Ashoka   third-century BCE northern-Indian king who was the first to embrace Buddhism

Atman   self

Bhikku   monk

Bodh gaya where Buddha attained enlightenment under a peepul tree, now called a bodhi tree

Bodhi enlightenment, in some Buddhist schools

Bodhidharma the first teacher of Ch'an buddhism, who founded the principal of paradox and question as in Zen

Bodhisattva (Mahayana Buddhism) one who has achieved enlightenment but remains in order to teach rather than attain nirvana

Bon the religion of Tibet before the advent of Buddhism, shamanistic, nature-worshipping

Buddha The Enlightened One. First the historical Buddha, Siddhartha Gotama. Second, anyone who has reached enlightenment

Buddhaghosa fifth-century CE writer of commentaries on the scriptures

Ch'an Chinese school of meditation

Dalai Lama worldly leader of Tibetan Buddhism, held to be a reincarnation of Avalokiteshvara

Dhamma/Dharma the Buddha's teachings

Dhammapada one of the texts of the Pali Canon, the essence of the Theravada teachings

Dharmas many meanings: (i) the one ultimate Reality; (ii) an ultimately real event; (iii) as reflected in life: righteousness, virtue; (iv) as interpreted in the Buddha's teaching: doctrine, scripture, Truth; (v) object of the sixth sense organ, i.e. of mind; (vi) property; (vii) mental state; (viii) thing; (ix) quality (from Buddhist scriptures)

Enlightenment the realization of the truth of all existence; the passing into nirvana thereby

Hinayana 'Little Vehicle', considered an insulting term for Theravada Buddhism, the doctrine of salvation for oneself alone

Honen 1133–1212 CE, Japanese teacher of Pure Land Buddhism

Hua-yen Chinese school which recognizes the interrelatedness of all things

Karma a volitional action which is either wholesome or unwholesome and in consequence is rewarded or punished

Jodo Japanese name for Pure Land Buddhism

Kegon   Japanese Buddhist school, *see* Hua-yen

Koan   technique of mind-bending questioning used in Rinzai Zen to bring about satori

Lama   Tibetan religious leader

Lotus Sutra   the scripture based on one of Buddha's speeches given to gods, demons, rulers and cosmic powers. The essence of Mahayana teachings and of the Chinese T'ien-t'ai and Japanese Tendai schools

Mahayana   'Great Vehicle', northern Buddhism, accepts the doctrine of the Bodhisattva

Mandala   concentric circles as a visual aid towards self-realization in Tibetan Buddhism

Mantra   a symbolic sound used in meditation as an aid to self-realization in Tibetan Buddhism

Mantrayana/Tantrayana/Vajrayana/Tibetan   the third form of Buddhism, best known as coming from Tibet

Maitreya   the Buddha to come

Mudra   symbolic gestures, used specially in Mantrayana Buddhism

Mu   Chinese for 'no-thing' or 'non-existence', often used in reference to Zen koans

Nichiren   1222–82 CE, ultra-nationalist Japanese reformer who considered that the Lotus Sutra contained the ultimate truth, denouncing all other Buddhisms

Nirvana/nibbana   a blowing out, a ceasing of self, liberation, extinction

Panchen Lama   the spiritual head of the Tibetan Buddhists, held to be a reincarnation of Amitabha

Pali Canon   the Theravadin Buddhist scriptures

Prayer wheels   on which are inscribed Om Mane Padme Hum, the turning of which increases the power of the prayer

Rinzai Zen   the school which uses koans to induce satori

Samsara   'stream of existence', Sanskrit word for the continuing cycle of birth and death and rebirth

Sangha   community of monks and nuns which started with Buddha's first disciples

Satori   sudden enlightenment in Zen

Shingon 'True Word' sect in Japan, influenced by Tantra and Shinto

Shinran 1173–1263 CE, disciple of Honen, founder of Jodo Shinsu sect

Skilful Means method of propounding the Dhamma in ways according to the ability of the hearers

Soto Zen a gradual realization of satori, the other Zen school

Sutra an authoritative text which is claimed to have been spoken by the Buddha

Sutta-pitaka basket of discourses, the most important Theravada scriptures

Theravada the Doctrine of the Elders, Southern Buddhism, rejects the doctrine of the bodhisattva

Three Refuges the Buddha, the Dhamma and the Sangha (also thought of as the Three Jewels and the core of the faith)

Tipitaka Pali (Sanskrit Tripitaka), the three baskets of Buddha's teachings in the Theravada canon

Vinaya-pitaka rules of discipline for the Sangha

Za-Zen form of Zen meditation

Zen a Japanese Buddhism from the Chinese Ch'an in the thirteenth century CE

JAINISM

Acaranga the first anga of the Shvetambara scriptural canon

Acarya leader of an ascetic group

Agama scriptural tradition

Ahimsa doctrine of non-violence

Ajiva unsentient existence

Anekantvada the doctrine of many-sidedness (or enormous tolerance)

Anga literally limb: the Shvetambara canon is divided into twelve angas, or limbs

Ardhamagadhi language of the Shvetembara scriptures

Asceticism austere practices which lead to control of mind and body, such as fasting, meditation, solitude

Caturmas the four-monthly monsoon retreat
Chedasutra Shvetambara text on rules of ascetic behaviour
Dana religious giving
Digambara literally 'sky-clad' or naked: one of the two major sects of Jainism
Drishtivada the lost canon of the Shvetambara scriptures
Fordmaker Tirthankara, one of the 24 teachers of the Jain doctrine
Jina conqueror, epithet of the fordmakers
Jiva soul
Kalika text only to be studied at specific times
Kaliyuga corrupt age
Kalpasutra the Shvetambara scriptures which contain the life of Mahavira
Mahavira Great Hero, name of the twenty-fourth Tirthankara
Mahavir Jayanti festival celebrating Mahavira's birthday
Muhpatti mouth-shield
Mula Sangha the 'Root Assembly', the most celebrated Digambara ascetic lineage
Obligatory Actions six actions incumbent on ascetics
Parshva the twenty-third fordmaker
Puja worship
Sallekhana religious death through fasting
Shravana Belgola most important Digembara holy place
Shvetambara literally 'white-clad', wearers of white robes: one of the two major sects of Jainism
Sthanakvasi Shvetambara non-image-worshipping sect
Terapanth Shvetambara non-image-worshipping sect
Three Jewels Right Faith, Right Knowledge and Right Practice
Tirtha Jain community
Upanga subsidiary scriptural text
Utkalika a text which can be studied at any time

SIKHISM

Adi Granth/Guru Granth Sahib the Sikh holy scriptures, the ultimate authority

Amrit   offering of water, blessed and sweetened with sugar

Amritsar   the site of the Golden Temple, built by Arjan, the fifth Guru, holy place of the Sikhs

Angad   limb, name given to second Guru

Ardas   daily prayer, literally 'petition'

Bhaiji   brother

Commensality   eating together to promote integration

Divali, Diwali   festival of lights, marks the release from prison of the sixth Guru

Granthi   person entrusted with the duties of the gurdwara

Guru Gobind Singh   the tenth and last Guru, who shifted authority from the Gurus to the Adi Granth, and who required all Sikh men to take a particular name, Singh, and wear distinctive clothing

Gurdwara   temple which houses the Adi Granth, and meeting place where a communal meal is held after worship

Gurmurkhi   Sikh script, founded by Angad, in which all scriptures and hymns are written

Gurpurb   festival commemorating the birth or death of a Guru

Guru   teacher, referring to the ten Gurus of the Sikh religion from Guru Nanak to Guru Gobind Singh

Harimandir   the House of God, the Golden Temple at Amritsar

Jap   meditation

Japji   confession of faith and daily prayer

Jore melas   festivals

Kaccha   see Khalsa

Kangha   see Khalsa

Kara   see Khalsa

Katha   explanation of hymn sung at worship

Kaur   Princess; name given to all Sikh women

Keshas   see Khalsa

Khalsa   (community)   originally the militant community organized by the tenth Guru. The five Ks are the traditional marks of the Khalsa: keshas – uncut hair, kangha – comb, kaccha – short breeches, kirpan – sword, and kara – bracelet

Kirpan   see Khalsa

Kirtan   hymn-singing at worship
Kshatriya   warrior class
Langar   communal meal after worship
Mul Mantra   the statement of belief composed by Guru Nanak
Nirankar   without form
Nirguna   without qualities
Panj pyare   beloved five, the original members of the Khalsa
Sangat   congregation
Satguru   Divine Teacher, literally True Preceptor

CONFUCIANISM

Analects   the essence of Confucius' teachings, one of the four books of the Confucian canon
Chia   philosophy
Chiao   religion
Chih   wisdom
Chung Yung   Doctrine of the Mean — the importance of a middle path in all things
Chu'n Ch'iu   Annals of Spring and Autumn, one of the Five Classics
Five Classics   the five books of the Confucian canon: Su Chung, I Ching, Shi Ching, Li Ching, and Ch'un Ch'iu
Five Virtues   jen, li, yi, chih, hsin
Hsin   good faith
Hsun Tzu   rational Chinese scholar of the third century BCE who meshed Confucianism and Taoism
I Ching   Book of Changes, one of the Five Classics, the book of divination
Kung Fu-Tzu   Chinese name for Confucius
Jen   benevolence
Ju   literally scolars, literati: Chinese word for Confucianism
Ju-chiao   Confucianism
Li   concept of propriety and reverence towards all, respect in all forms, manners
Li-chaio   Confucianism
Li Ching   Book of Rites, one of the Five Classics

Lun yu Analects of Confucius
Meng Tzu, Mencius b.371 BCE. Developed the teachings of Confucius
Mohism a theory of universal and unconditional love
Shi Ching Book of Odes, one of the Five Classics
Su Ching Book of History, one of the Five Classics
Tien ming the Will of Heaven
Ta Hsueh Book of Great Learning
Yi duty

TAOISM

Ch'i breath, vitality
Ching essence
Feng Shui geomancy, the divination of place, the art of positioning buildings (and graves) to take account of all polarities and life forces
I Ching Book of Changes, book of divinatory hexagrams, part of the Confucian canon
Shen spirit
T'ai–chi immortal, primordial breath, the 'totally transcendent'
Tao the Way, the underlying principle of unity
Tao te Ching work ascribed to Lao Tzu
Te virtue
Wu not being
Yang chi breath of heaven
Yin chi breath of earth
Yin and Yang the principles of opposites, polarities of energies, the feminine-masculine principle of dark/light, bad/good, etc.
Yu being

SHINTO

Amaterasu Sun Goddess, the principal deity of Shinto. All Emperors claimed descent from Amaterasu
Animism the theory that natural objects and phenomena have souls

Harae   exorcism

Imi   abstinence

Ise   one of the major shrines of Japan

Izanagi   the Sky god, father of Amaterasu, the male principle

Izanami   the Earth Goddess, the female principle, who with Izanagi created the islands of Japan

Izumo   one of the major shrines of Japan

Kami   beneficent forces of nature and spirits associated mostly with fertility and growth, from which the Japanese nation is 'descended'

Kojiki/Koniki   Record of Ancient Matters: myths and legends of Japanese creation, etc, the oldest of the Shinto scriptures

Matsuri   ceremonies, festivals

Miko   shaman

Nihongi/Nihon Shoki   written chronicles of Japan, containing creation myths

Pollution   that which dirties, either literally and physically as in mud or faeces, or mentally and spiritually as when bad thoughts and deeds pollute the mind

Samurai   warrior

Shintai   the 'god-body' – the representation of the god in the shrine

Shogatsu   New Year festival

Shogun   feudal ruler

Susano-o   the Withering Wind, the principle of pollution

PRIMAL RELIGIONS

Ancestors   the majority of primal religions venerate ancestors, who play a large part in mediation between the living and the dead

Animism   the belief that souls reside in natural objects and phenomena

Bull-roarer   see Storyboards

Cargo cults   new religious movements occurring (mostly) in Melanesia, in which believers expect both deliverance by a messiah and corresponding material wealth

Dreamtime the age when the Australian Aboriginal ancestors created the features of the earth. Today the fables are recreated in dance, art and other ceremonies

Exorcism the driving out of evil spirits by ritual or prayer

Fetishism belief and reverence for an object supposed either to be imbued with special powers or in which a particular spirit resides

Polytheism belief in many gods who rule over the many and varied aspects of daily life

Ritual set pattern in religious ceremonies. Mythical stories told through dance or drama relating to the continuance and prosperity of the community

Sacrifice a ritual offering (animal or vegetable) to the gods, made for various reasons, such as gratitude, or for favours or divination, or as an expression of communion. In some cultures live sacrifice is still evident

Shaman present in many cultures, is likened (often wrongly) to a medicine man or a witch doctor, but is distinguished by his ability to enter a trance and thus communicate with the gods, spirits, elements and ghosts by travelling to other and insubstantial worlds

Storyboards stones and boards on which patterns representing the myths and genus of the Australian Aborigines are scratched. Used by the older men of the tribes who are skilled both in interpretation and telling

Taboo, tabu, tapu Polynesian word meaning prohibited, not allowed. Also in the sense of separate, therefore with divine intent. Has passed into the English language in its original sense

BIBLIOGRAPHY

GENERAL READING

Six Religions in the Twentieth Century, W. Owen Cole with Peggy Moran, Hulton Educational Publications Ltd, Cheltenham, 1984

The World's Religions, Ninian Smart, Press Syndicate of the University of Cambridge, Cambridge, 1989

Festivals in World Religions, ed. Alan Brown, Longman Group Ltd, London, 1986

Religious Leaders, Jacques Brosse, W&R Chambers Ltd, Edinburgh, 1991 (First published in France as *Les maîtres spirituels*, Bordas, Paris, 1988)

Hutchinson Encyclopedia of Living Faiths, ed. R.C. Zaehner, Random Century Group, London, 1991

A Handbook of Living Religions, ed. John R. Hinnells, Penguin Books, Harmondsworth, 1984

A Lion Handbook: The World's Religions, Lion Publishing plc, Oxford, 1994

The Penguin Dictionary of Religions, ed. John R. Hinnells, Penguin Books, Harmondsworth, 1984

The Archeology of World Religions: the Background of Primitivism, Hinduism, Jainism, Buddhism, Confucianism, Tao, Shinto, Islam and Sikhism, Jack Finegan, Princeton University Press, Princeton, 1952

Encyclopedia of World Religions, Octopus Books, London, 1975

JUDAISM

Judaism, Isidore Epstein, Penguin Books, Harmondsworth, 1959 (reprinted 1990)

Major Trends in Jewish Mysticism, Gershom G. Scholem, Schocken Books Inc, New York, 1961

Elements of Judaism, Brian Lancaster, Element Books, Shaftesbury, 1993

The Kabbalah Unveiled, translated into English from the Latin version of Knorr von Rosenroth and collated with original Chaldean and Hebrew text, S.L. MacGregor Mathers, Arkana, Penguin Books, Harmondsworth, 1991

Judaism, Jan Thompson, Edward Arnold, London, 1980

Magic and the Qabbalah, W.E. Butler, Aquarian Press, Northampton, 1978

Judaism, Arthur Herzberg, Prentice Hall, New York, 1962

Judaism, Nicholas de Lange, Oxford University Press, Oxford, 1986

The Judaic Law, William Corlett, Hamish Hamilton, London, 1979

CHRISTIANITY

The Early Church, W.H.C. Frend, SCM Press, London, 1965

The Early Church, H. Chadwick, vol.1, Pelican History of the Church, Penguin Books, Harmondsworth, 1960

Early Christianity, ed. Ian Hazlett, SPCK, London, 1991

Augustine of Hippo, Peter Brown, Faber & Faber, London, 1967

A History of the English Church and People, Bede, revised, ed. R.E. Latham, Penguin Books, Harmondsworth, 1968

The Orthodox Church, Kallistos T. Ware, Penguin Books, Harmondsworth, 1963

Religion and the Decline of Magic, Keith Thomas, Penguin Books, Harmondsworth, 1971

The Reformation, O. Chadwick, vol. 3, Pelican History of the Church, Penguin Books, Harmondsworth, reprinted 1992

Mere Christianity, C.S. Lewis, Macmillan, London, 1952

On Being a Christian, Hans Kung, Collins, London, 1976

The Gospel, Then and Now, A.M. Hunter, SCM Press, London, 1978

Return to the Centre, Bede Griffiths, Collins, London, 1976

The Phenomenon of Christianity, Ninian Smart, Collins, London, 1979

The Heart of the Matter, Teilard de Chardin, tr. from French Rene Hague, Collins, London, 1978

Myth and Ritual in Christianity, Alan Watts, Thames and Hudson, London, 1954

Dark Night of the Soul, St. John of the Cross, tr. from Spanish E. Allison Peers, Burns & Oates, Tunbridge Wells, 1976

ISLAM

Understanding Islam, Frithjof Schuon, Mandala Books, Allen and Unwin, London, 1963

Elements of Islam, Shaykh Fadhlalla Haeri, Element Books, Shaftesbury, 1993

Elements of Sufism, Shaykh Fadhlalla Haeri, Element Books, Shaftesbury, 1990

The Koran, translated with notes by N.J. Dawood, Penguin Books, Harmondsworth, 1956

Discovering Islam, Akbar S. Ahmed, Routledge & Kegan Paul, London, 1988

Islam, Alfred Guillaume, Penguin Books, Harmondsworth, 1954

Muslim Saints and Mystics: Episodes from the Tadhkirat al-Auliya, Farid al-Din Attar, tr. A.J. Arberry, Arkana, Penguin Books, Harmondsworth, 1990

Ideals and Realities of Islam, Seyyad Hossein Nasr, Aquarian Press, London, 1994

Introduction to Islam, Frederick M.Denny, Macmillan, London, 1994

Koran Interpreted, A.J. Arberry, HarperCollins, London 1981

Selections from the Koran, Sirdar Ikbal Ali Shah, Octagon Press, London, 1980

The Tradition of Islam, Introduction to the Study of Hadith Literature, Alfred Guillaume, Curzon Press, London, 1993

The Last Barrier, Reshad Feild, Element Books, Shaftesbury, 1993

BAHÁ'Í

The Elements of the Bahá'í Faith, Joseph Sheppherd, Element Books, Shaftesbury, 1992

Gleanings of the Writings of Baha'u'llah, tr. Shogi Effendi, Bahá'í Publishing Trust, 1983

The Babi and Bahá'í Religions, Peter Smith, Cambridge University Press, Cambridge, 1981

A Short History of Bahá'í, Peter Smith, Oneworld Publications, Oxford, 1995

ZOROASTRIANISM

The Teachings of the Magi, A Compendium of Zoroastrian Beliefs, R.C. Zaehner, Sheldon Press, London, 1975

Zoroastrians, Their Religious Beliefs and Practices, Mary Boyce, Routledge & Kegan Paul, London, 1979

Dawn and Twilight of Zoroastrianism, R.C. Zaehner, Weidenfeld & Nicolson, London, 1961

The Zoroastrian Tradition, An Introduction to the Ancient Wisdom of Zarathustra, Farhang Nehr, Element Books, Shaftesbury, 1991

HINDUISM

The Elements of Hinduism, Stephen Cross, Element Books, Shaftesbury, 1994

Yoga: Immortality and Freedom, Mircea Eliade, Princeton, 1969

Hinduism, R.C. Zaehner, Oxford University Press, Oxford, 1966

The Bhagavad Gita As It Is, His Divine Grace A.C. Bhaktivedanta Swami Prabhupada, Bhaktivedanta Book Trust, International Society for Krishna Consciousness, Borehamwood, Herts, 1983

The Geeta, The Gospel of Lord Shri Krishna, Shri Purohit Swami, Faber & Faber, London, 1965

Bhagavadgita, tr. Sir Edwin Arnold, Constable & Co, London, 1993

The Wonder that was India, A.L. Basham, Fontana, London, 1971

The Hindu Religious Tradition, P. Bowes, Routledge and Kegan Paul, London, 1978

Hindu Myths, tr. from the Sanskrit, ed. Wendy Doniger O'Flaherty, Penguin Books, Harmondsworth, 1975

Autobiography of a Yogi, Paramahansa Yogananda, Rider & Company, London, 1950

JAINISM

The Jains, Paul Dundas, ed. John Hinnells and Ninian Smart, Routledge, London, 1992

Jainism and ..., Vinod Kapashi, Mrs Sudha Kapashi, Middlesex, 1991

BUDDHISM

Buddhism, Holly Connolly and Peter Connolly, World Religions Series, ed. W. Owen Cole, Stanley Thornes Publishers, Cheltenham, 1989

The Teachings of the Compassionate Buddha, E.A. Burtt, New American Library, New York, 1955

The Life of the Buddha in Legend and History, E.J. Thomas, Routledge & Kegan Paul, London, 1949

What the Buddha Taught, W .Rahula, Gordon Fraser, Bedford, 1959

What the Buddha Never Taught, Timothy Ward, Element Books, Shaftesbury, 1990

In the Tracks of Buddhism, Frithjof Schuon, Allen & Unwin, London, 1968

The Buddha: Buddhist Civilization in India & Ceylon, Trevor Ling, Temple Smith, London, 1973

The Buddha, Michael Carrithers, Oxford University Press, Oxford, 1983

Buddhism, Trevor Ling, Ward Lock Educational, W. Sussex, 1970

Mahayana Buddhism, Beatrice Lane Suzuki, Unwin, London, 1990

A Short History of Buddhism, Edward Conze, Oneworld Publications, Oxford, 1993

A Popular Dictionary of Buddhism, Christmas Humphreys, Curzon Press, London, 1976

Studies in the Middle Way, Christmas Humphreys, Curzon Press, London, 1976

The Way of Action: the Buddha's Way to Enlightenment, Christmas Humphreys, Allen & Unwin, London, 1960

Walk On, Christmas Humphries, Buddhist Society, London, 1947

A Technique of Living – based on Buddhist psychological principles, Leonard A. Bullen, Buddhist Publication Society, Sri Lanka, 1982

The Buddha's Way, Hammalawa Sadhatissa, Allen & Unwin, London, 1971

Buddhism, Christmas Humphreys, Penguin Books, Harmondsworth, 1962

Buddhism, John Snelling, Element Books, Shaftesbury, 1990

Journey of Insight Meditation: a personal experience of the Buddha's Way, Eric Lerner, Turnstone Press, London, 1978

The Diamond Sutra and the Heart Sutra, tr. Edward Conze, Buddhist Wisdom Books, Allen & Unwin, London, 1958, 1975

The Dhammapada, Eknath Easwaran, Routledge & Kegan Paul, London, 1986

The Dhammapada, Jack Austin, Buddhist Society, London, 1945

The Discourse Collection: Selected Texts from the Sutta Nipata, tr. John Ireland, Buddhist Publication Society, Sri Lanka, 1965

Buddhist Scriptures, Selected and tr. by Edward Conze, Penguin Books, Harmondsworth, 1959

The Sound of One Hand: 281 Zen Koans with Answers, tr. Yoel Hoffman, Sheldon Press, London, 1975

A Zen Wave: Basho's Haiku & Zen, Robert Aitken, John Weatherhill Inc, New York, 1978

Zen Dictionary, Ernest Wood, Penguin Books, Harmondsworth, 1977

The Spirit of Zen: a way of life, work, and art in the far east, Alan W. Watts, Grove Press Inc, New York, 1960

The Way of Zen, Alan W. Watts, Pelican, Penguin Books, Harmondsworth, 1962

Essays in Zen Buddhism, Second Series, D.T. Suzuki, Rider Books, London, 1950

Introduction to Zen Buddhism, D.T. Suzuki, ed. Christmas Humphrey, introduction by C.G. Jung, Rider Books Ltd, London, 1991

The Method of Zen, Eugene Herrigel, tr. R.F.C. Hull, Arkana, Penguin Books, Harmondsworth 1988

Zen Mind, Beginner's Mind, Shunryu Suzuki, John Weatherhill Inc, New York, 1970

The Tibetan Book of Living and Dying, Sogyal Rinpoche, ed. Patrick Jaffney and Andrew Harvey, Rider Books, 1995

The Miracle of Mindfulness: a manual of meditation, Thich Nhat Hanh, Rider Books Ltd, London, 1991

Compassion Yoga: Mystical Cult of Kuan Yin, John Blofeld, Mandala Books, London 1977

The Tibetan Book of the Dead, the Great Liberation through Hearing in the Bardo, Guru Rinpoche according to Karma Lingpa, tr. & commentary by Francesca Freemantle and Chogyam Trungpa, Shambala Books, California, 1975

Born in Tibet, Chogyam Trungpa, Penguin Books, Harmondsworth, 1971

The Way of Power: A Practical Guide to the Tantric Mysticism of Tibet, J.J. Blofeld, Allen & Unwin, London, 1970

SIKHISM

Sikhism, Piara Singh Sambhi, World Religions Series, ed.
W. Owen Cole, Stanley Thornes Publishers, Cheltenham,
1989

The Sikhs: Their Religious Beliefs and Practices, W.O. Cole
and P.S. Sambhi, Routledge & Kegan Paul, London, 1978

Sikhism, Sue Penney, Heinemann Ltd, London, 1997

Sikhism, Beryl Dhanjal, Batsford Ltd, 1987

Adi Granth, Selections from the Sacred Writings of the Sikhs,
Allen & Unwin, London, 1960

Teach Yourself Sikhism, W. Owen Cole, Hodder & Stoughton,
London, 1994

CONFUCIUS

Confucius in Life and Legend, Betty Kelen, Sheldon Press
London, 1974

Confucius and Confucianism, Richard Wilhelm, tr. by George
H. Dante and Annina Periam Dante, Routledge & Kegan
Paul, London, 1972

Analects, tr. from Chinese and Introduction by D.C. Lau,
Penguin Books, Harmondsworth, 1979

Confucius – Analects, ed. Raymond Dawson, World's Classics
Series, Oxford University Press, Oxford, 1993

Three Ways of Thought in Ancient China, Arthur Waley,
Allen & Unwin, London, 1939

TAOISM

The Tao: A Way of Being, Stanley Rosenthal, S. Rosenthal,
Cardiff, 1977

The Way and its Power, Arthur Waley, Allen & Unwin,
London, 1937

Tao: the Watercourse Way, Alan Watts, With Al Chung-liang
Huang, Pantheon Books, New York, 1975

The Tao is Silent, Raymond M. Smullyan, Harper & Row, New York, 1977
   Alan W.Watts, Abacus, Sphere Books, London, 1977
Cloud Hidden, Whereabouts Unknown: A Mountain Journal, Alan W. Watts, Abacus, Sphere Books, London, 1977
Tao te Ching, Lao-tzu, tr. Gia-fu Feng and Jane English, Wildwood House, London, 1973
Chang Tsu: Inner Chapters, tr. Gia-fu Feng and Jane English, Wildwood House, London, 1974

SHINTO

Shinto and the State, Helen Hardacre, Princeton University Press, Princeton, 1989
The Sacred East: Hinduism, Buddhism, Confucianism, Taoism, Shinto, Macmillan Books, London, 1996
Ancestor Worship in Contemporary Japan, R.J. Smith, Stanford University Press, California, 1974

PRIMAL RELIGIONS – NORTH AMERICA

Touch the Earth, ed. T.C. McLuhan, Pocket Books, New York, 1971

INDEX